EXPERIMENTING WITH ELECTRICITY AND MAGNETISM

BY OVID K. WONG

A VENTURE BOOK
FRANKLIN WATTS
NEW YORK   CHICAGO   LONDON   TORONTO   SYDNEY

On the cover: A Van de Graaf generator (courtesy of the Museum of Science, Boston).

Photographs copyright © : Archive Photos, NYC: pp. 13 (Lambert), 36 top (Dean); Patsy Kelley: p. 17; Photo Researchers, Inc.: pp. 18 (Will & Deni McIntyre), 36 bottom (SPL), 70 (Andrew McClenaghan), 85 (SPL); The Bettmann Archive: p. 27; American Museum of Natural History, Library Services/Lee Boltin (neg# 322264): p. 27 inset; Randy Matusow: p. 53; Con Edison: p. 101.

Library of Congress Cataloging-in-Publication Data

Wong, Ovid K.
    Experimenting with electricity and magnetism / by Ovid K. Wong.
      p.   cm.—(A Venture book)
    Includes bibliographical references and index.
    Summary: Provides instructions for a variety of simple experiments demonstrating the principles and properties of electricity and magnetism.
    ISBN 0-531-12547-5
    1. Electricity—Juvenile literature.   2. Magnetism—Juvenile literature.   3. Electricity—Experiments—Juvenile literature.
4. Magnetism—Experiments—Juvenile literature. [1. Electricity—Experiments. 2. Magnetism—Experiments. 3. Experiments.]
I. Title.
QC527.2.W65   1993
537'.078—dc20   92-37672   CIP   AC

This book is dedicated
to the thirty-five
Honors Science Teachers
of Illinois (1989–91)
for their inspiration,
collegiality, and friendship.

CONTENTS

FOREWORD

Electricity is an amazing physical concept! This idea has intrigued mankind for at least twenty-six hundred years. An ancient Greek philosopher, Thales, observed that amber would attract small objects after being rubbed. The charged amber exerted force over a distance like magnetism. In fact, the Greek word for amber is *electron*. People have been studying electricity ever since.

Dr. Ovid K. Wong in his eighth science book addresses this amazing commodity, electricity. There are ample opportunities for young scientists to test ideas, gather data, draw conclusions, and apply principles in new and diverse situations. This book presents the historical flow of electricity and magnetism over time, but it goes well beyond mere description. You will be stimulated by experiments, the hands-on approach to investigations, which are both challenging and exciting.

The main idea to remember is this: We do not know "all about" this topic yet. There are wondrous discoveries yet to be made with new and undiscovered applications awaiting the curious and questioning mind.

This book presents a springboard to new thinking. Trade new lamps for old ones as you go beyond the known and into the unknown realm. Remember these sage words of the American chemist Albert Szent-Györgyi (1893–1986):

Discovery consists in seeing what everybody has seen and thinking what nobody has thought.

Happy Discovering!

Thomas C. Fitch, Ph.D.,
the Distinguished Professor
of Science Education,
Illinois State University,
Normal, Illinois

INTRODUCTION: ELECTRICITY AND MAGNETISM

Although seemingly different, electricity and magnetism are actually two forms of the same force. It's important to remember that statement as you experience the many experiments in this book. The relationship between electricity and magnetism can be stated simplistically: whenever electricity moves, magnetism is produced; whenever a magnetic force field changes, electricity is produced.

We are not usually aware of electrical effects when we use magnets in our daily lives; nor are we aware of magnetic fields when we use electricity. Unfortunately, like other forces, electric and magnetic forces are invisible. If only we could see or feel electric and magnetic forces, and know they were there without needing to use special detecting instruments, their close relationship would become obvious to us because we would find them always acting together.

Experiments in this book are clustered under specific topics of interest. Beginning experiments are typically simple, while projects and invention activities are more challenging. Welcome to the wonderful world of experimenting with electricity and magnetism!

A Note About Safety

Please remember the following important safety rules:

1.   Do not experiment with electricity from wall outlets. Household electricity is dangerous and can kill you.

2.   Never work with lights or appliances that are plugged into a wall outlet.

3.   Avoid downed power lines and electric company substations. They are extremely dangerous.

4.   Wear safety glasses when cutting metal and when working with hot or corrosive liquids (including soldering).

1

ELECTRICITY
AT REST

You have probably experienced electrical effects like these: You scuffed your shoes across a nylon carpet and then created a spark by touching a doorknob. You unfolded nylon clothing taken from a clothes dryer and noticed a crackling noise and sparks. These and many other examples indicate the presence of electricity transferred by the frictional contact between objects. Electricity produced by friction can be stored on the surface of nonconducting substances such as rubber, glass, and cloth materials. This type of electrical charge buildup is known as static electricity. *Static* means non-moving. If static electricity remained static we might never notice it, but it doesn't. When you saw a spark when touching a doorknob or heard a snap when unfolding clothing you were actually seeing or hearing static electricity in motion. Static electricity makes sparks when it jumps. The branch of physics that studies electricity at rest is known as electrostatics.

The spectacular display of lightning in thunderstorms is a good example of powerful electrical movement in the atmosphere caused by the buildup and discharge of electric charges. On hot, humid days, heavy clouds become charged with static electricity. Typically, positive charges tend to build up at the top of the cloud and negative charges move to the bottom. Eventually, a heavy charge builds up and the negative electrons discharge, or jump, in an attempt to balance themselves. The air gets very hot. This causes the flash of lightning, accompanied by the shock wave of pressure that we hear as thunder.

HISTORY

Benjamin Franklin ● Most Americans know Benjamin Franklin (1706–1790) as a hero of the Revolution, a prominent statesman, and a Founding Father. However, Franklin, a self-made man who achieved wealth and fame through determination and intelligence, was also a scientist who made important contributions to the understanding of static electricity.

Franklin's best-known discovery is that lightning is caused by discharges of static electricity in the atmo-

12

Buildup of electric charge in the atmosphere, especially on hot, humid days, causes lightning.

sphere. To test his hypothesis, he conducted his famous kite experiment. He flew the kite during a thunderstorm using conducting silk thread as the string. Attached to the silk kite string was a metal key. Franklin found that electric charges from the atmosphere traveled through the silk thread to the metal key. In this dangerous experiment, Franklin diverted some of the deadly electricity through the key into the earth. The immediate practical result of Franklin's work was his invention of the first lightning conductor, a device that safely diverts intense electric charges from buildings, thereby preventing the loss of life and property. The lightning conductor is still widely used today.

Henry Cavendish ● The British scientist Henry Cavendish (1731–1810) is known for his outstanding work in electricity. His earlier research established basic concepts for understanding the nature of electricity. In his experiments he defined the nature of electric force as the attraction and repulsion existing between two charged bodies. These forces play a key role in explaining electrostatic phenomena.

Charles Coulomb ● The French physicist Charles Coulomb (1736–1806) formulated the law that describes the forces that exist between electric charges. The law states that like charges repel and opposite charges attract, and that a force exists between any two charged objects. That force is proportional to the product of the two charges divided by the square of the distance between them. Thus Coulomb's law is expressed as

$$F = k(Q_1 \times Q_2) / d^2$$

where F is the force, Q1 and Q2 are the charges, d is the distance between them, and k is a constant.

BACKGROUND INFORMATION

Electricity is closely related to the atomic structure of matter. Everything in the universe is made of very small particles called atoms. You are made of atoms; so are the chairs and tables in your home, the food that you eat, and the air that you breathe. Each atom is so small that it takes millions of them to form the head of a straight pin, for example. An atom has a positively charged nucleus in the center surrounded by negatively charged electrons in orbits. The sum total charge of an atom is always neutral because the positive and negative charges equal and cancel each other. The movement of "loose" electrons in orbits causes atoms to gain or lose one or more electrons. Consequently, atoms gaining one or more electrons will become negatively charged while atoms losing one or more electrons will become positively charged. Keep in mind that electricity is the result of moving electrons. Can you mathematically visualize how the movement of the negatively charged electrons affects the total charge of a neutrally charged atom?

Static electricity is produced in various materials by rubbing them with other substances. These materials build up either negative or positive charges, depending on whether they gain or lose electrons. As we know from Coulomb's law, substances of opposite charge attract each other. Conversely, substances of the same charge repel each other. When wool and plastic are rubbed together, electrons can be made to move from one to the other. The atoms in the plastic pick up some loose electrons from the atoms in the wool. There are now extra electrons on the plastic, so it is no longer balanced but negatively charged. The wool has lost electrons so it too is no longer balanced; the larger number of protons than electrons makes it positively charged. The wool and the plastic will attract each other because unlike charges attract.

EXPERIMENT 1: What Are the Effects of Electrostatic Charges?

Materials ● Ne2 neon light bulb (from an electronic hobby store), zip-lock plastic sandwich bag, newspaper strips

Procedure ● (see Figure 1)

1.   Spread the leads of the neon light bulb so that they point in opposite directions.
2.   Place the bulb inside the plastic bag and seal (zip-lock) the opening.
3.   Rub one side of the plastic bag with a silk cloth in a dark place (for example a closet).
4.   What do you see? Can you explain what happened?

(*Hint:* Rubbing will cause one side of the bag to become positively charged, the other side negatively charged.) Here is another simple experiment to determine the effects of electrostatic charges:

Materials ● Old newspaper, television set, wool blanket, miscellaneous objects found in your home

16

Two spherical terminals mounted on insulating columns are the basis of this high-voltage electrostatic generator, called a Van de Graaf generator, at the Museum of Science in Boston.

Young girl with a static electricity generator

Procedure ●

1.   Cut a strip of newspaper about 3 cm wide and 20 cm long.

2.   Hold the paper strip and bring its free end to the screen of a turned-on television. What happens to the paper? Can you explain why it behaves as it does?

3.   Move around your home with the paper strip.

18

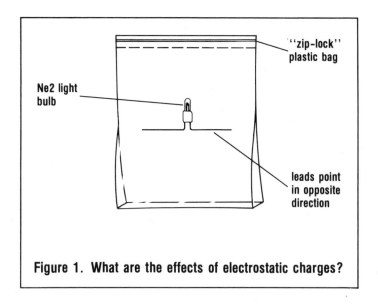

"zip-lock" plastic bag

Ne2 light bulb

leads point in opposite direction

Figure 1. What are the effects of electrostatic charges?

Bring it close to a windowpane, a wool blanket, or other items that you think of. Can you explain how the paper strip may be used to detect static electricity?

Time to Think ●

- If you charge a balloon by rubbing it with wool, the balloon will stick to a wall but not to a metal door. Can you offer an explanation?
- Two charged balls, A and B, are separated by a distance of 2 cm. The charge of ball A is 2 coulombs; B's charge is 8 coulombs. What is the force exerted between the two balls? Apply Coulomb's law of static electricity.
- Static electricity is most easily created on a cool, dry day. Can you figure out why?

EXPERIMENT 2: How Can a Homemade Electroscope Be Used to Detect Charges?

An electroscope is built in this activity. The instrument is later used to detect static electric charges.

Materials ● Old audio tape, two aluminum soda cans, metal cutter, masking tape, sandpaper, sharp knife, plastic pen with a smooth barrel, work gloves

Procedure ● (see Figure 2: Making an Electroscope)

1. For safety be sure an adult is helping or supervising while you do this step. Put on work gloves and use the metal cutter (heavy-duty scissors) to cut away the top and bottom of an aluminum soda can. The work gloves will protect your hands against sharp metal edges.

2. Flatten the can into a rectangle. Nip the corners as shown.

3. Fold it in half again the other way. Nip the corners with the metal cutter as shown.

4. Open the can and fold it into a four-sided frame. When it is viewed from the open ends it should look like a box with the two side walls missing.

5. Cut an X on top of the frame with the knife. (Be careful to avoid cutting yourself.) Push in the tabs and fold them to make a smooth square hole.

6. From the old audio tape, cut off a length of about 25 cm.

7. Cut a strip of aluminum from the can about the width of the audio tape and about 15 cm long. Use a piece of sandpaper to remove the coating from one side

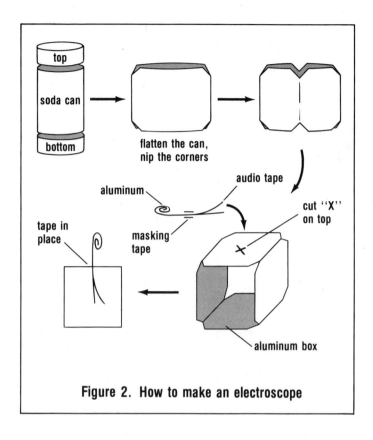

Figure 2. How to make an electroscope

of the aluminum strip. Roll one end of the strip until about 4 cm is unrolled.

8. Cut a short strip of the audio tape and fasten that to the unrolled end of the aluminum strip with a piece of masking tape. Make sure that the dull side of the tape faces the sanded side of the aluminum.

9. Hang the piece in the center of the hole with the help of tapes. The rolled end should be outside, and the end with the audio tape should be inside. Now you have successfully constructed a simple model of an electro-

scope. This instrument is used in the following steps to detect static electric charges.

10. Obtain a plastic pen with a smooth barrel and end. Rub the pen with a piece of fibrous cloth (*note*: a sweater sleeve will do). Immediately bring the smooth end (not the writing tip) of the pen near the rolled part of the electroscope.

11. Observe the audio tape and the aluminum strip inside the electroscope. What happens? Can you use the electric charge theory of attraction and repulsion to explain what you saw?

Time to Think ●

Before anything happens the electroscope is neutral. That means that the number of positive and negative charges are equal. When the plastic pen is rubbed with a piece of fibrous cloth, the pen is loaded with extra movable negative charges. What will happen to the distribution of charges on the aluminum strip and the audio tape when the pen is brought near the electroscope? Can you use a simple diagram to illustrate your explanation?

EXPERIMENT 3: What Is Electric Induction?

Materials ● Grains of puffed rice or wheat (from a cereal box), thread, large glass test tube, piece of silk cloth

Procedure ●

1. Hang a grain of puffed wheat or puffed rice by a thread.

2. Bring the large glass test tube close to, but not

close enough to touch, the grain. Can you describe what happens?

3.   Rub the test tube with the silk cloth. Again bring the test tube near the grain. Can you describe what happens?

Time to Think ● Can you hypothesize the electric charge (positive or negative) of the grain? Can you hypothesize the electric charge of the test tube before and after rubbing it with silk? How do the answers help you to understand electrical induction?

EXPERIMENT 4: How Does a Charged Object Affect Other Objects?

Materials ● Plastic wrap, sheet of paper towel, ruler, paper clip, salt, pepper, small pieces of aluminum foil, Styrofoam pieces

Procedure ●

1.   Place the paper clip, salt, pepper, aluminum foil, and Styrofoam on one side of a table, leaving as much space as possible between them.

2.   Place a piece of plastic wrap flat on the other side of the table. Rub it with the paper towel to create static electric charges.

3.   Predict what will happen when the wrap is brought to about 3 cm of the small objects you placed on the table. Record your predictions on the chart that follows.

4.   Hold and stretch the plastic wrap flat above each of the objects in turn. Record your observations on the chart.

Objects	Predictions	Observations
Paper clip	_____	_____
Salt	_____	_____
Pepper	_____	_____
Aluminum foil pieces	_____	_____
Styrofoam pieces	_____	_____

Time to Think ●

- Why did the plastic wrap pick up some objects but not others?
- What are the differences between your predictions and observations? What did you learn?
- How does a statically charged object affect other objects?

2

NATURE'S
ELECTRICITY

Because we are so familiar with man-made sources of electricity such as batteries, power generators, and the like, we often are surprised to learn that Mother Nature also generates electricity. Have you seen or used a gas grill pilot igniter? How does the igniter spark a flame? When you click the button of the lighter, the sparks that result are produced not by the rubbing of a flint but by the deformation of a crystal. The igniter and other sophisticated devices such as microphones, phonograph pickups, musical toys, smoke detector buzzers, tone generators in watches, ultrasonic cleaning devices, and ultrasonic submarine detectors are all examples of the use of piezoelectricity in our everyday lives. Piezoelectricity is produced by piezoelectric substances such as naturally occurring crystals.

HISTORY

In 1880, the French chemists Pierre and Jacques Curie discovered that electricity could be produced by various naturally occurring substances, such as crystals of quartz and tourmaline. They found that when these piezoelectric crystals change form under pressure, electricity is produced. Interestingly, the physical change in shape is not permanent because the same effect can be produced repeatedly. And conversely when electricity is applied to a piezoelectric crystal, that crystal will vibrate and change size. Another way of looking at this interesting phenomenon is in terms of converting energy from one form to another and back again. That is, in piezoelectric substances, mechanical energy will change to electrical energy, and in turn electrical energy will be converted back to mechanical energy.

Just what causes piezoelectricity in some naturally occurring crystals is not fully understood.

EXPERIMENT 5: How Can Piezoelectricity Be Generated?

Materials • Safety glasses, piezoelectric disk, Ne2 neon light bulb, speaker wire, solder, soldering iron, alligator clips, hammer

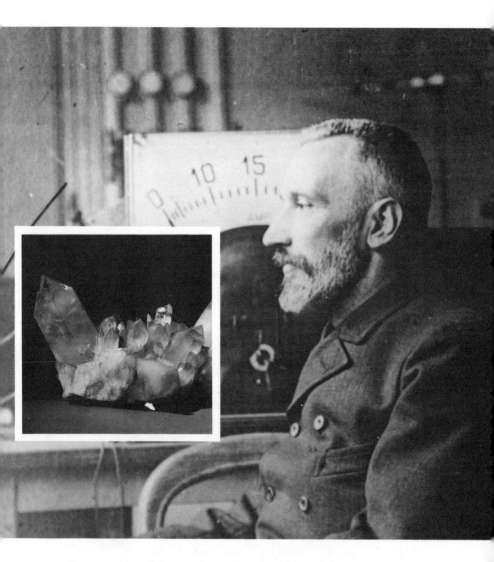

Pierre Curie (1859–1906), French scientist. He and his brother Jacques did extensive research on piezoelectricity. One of their discoveries was that quartz crystals (inset) could produce electricity.

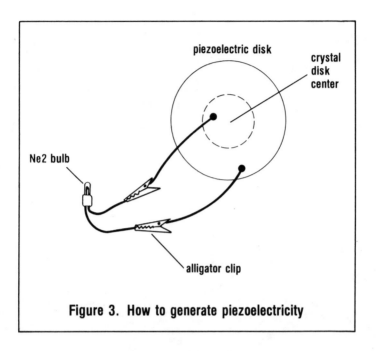

Figure 3. How to generate piezoelectricity

Procedure ● (see Figure 3)

1.   Obtain a flat piezoelectric disk either from a science supply store or from an old radio or other electric device that is ready to be thrown out. The metal disk has a crystal disk center. Treat the disk with great care; do not twist it. A damaged disk will not work in the experiment. An Ne2 neon light bulb can be obtained from a science supply or electrical store. The bulb is used because of its low voltage.

2.   **Put on safety glasses.** Solder the leads from a 30-cm-long speaker wire to the disk. Be careful not to inhale the harmful fumes from the soldering, and re-

member that a soldering iron gets very hot. One end of the wire should be soldered to the center of the disk. The other end should be soldered to the rim of the disk. (See Figure 3 for soldering locations.)

3. Connect the leads from the neon bulb to the two ends of the speaker wire not attached to the piezoelectric disk. Check all the wire connections.

4. Place the disk on a smooth, hard surface.

5. Hammer the center of the disk with a sharp, steady blow.

6. What happens to the neon light bulb? Can you explain?

Time to Think • Can you explain what you saw based on the piezoelectric theory?

EXPERIMENT 6: How Do You Light a Barbecue Gas Lighter?

Materials • Barbecue gas lighter (e.g., a Scripto Aim Flame), Ne2 neon bulb

Procedure •

1. Depress the trigger of a barbecue gas lighter several times to get a flame. Do you hear a rather distinct *click*? Do you hear the sound before seeing the flame or vice versa?

2. Carefully insert one lead of the Ne2 neon light bulb into the butane orifice. Let the other end of the lead hang over the side to touch the metallic outer frame of the lighter.

3. Remove the butane cartridge. Depress the trigger.

What happens to the neon bulb? Do you recognize any similarities between this activity and the previous one?

Time to Think ●

Did you hear a rather loud *click* when you depressed the trigger of the gas lighter? Is a flint and striker wheel used to light the butane gas? Are batteries needed for this lighter?

EXPERIMENT 7: How Does the Patio Gas Grill Igniter Work?

Materials ● A replacement gas grill igniter (from a hardware store)

Procedure ●

1.   Identify the different parts of a gas grill igniter. These parts are the red button, the black housing which is the body of the device, the red wire, and the insulated metal lead from the housing.
2.   Hold the insulated end of the red wire and the black housing in each hand. Bring the end of the red wire close to the insulated metal lead, but not close enough to touch.
3.   Depress the red button. What do you see?

Time to Think ●

What could be inside the housing of the igniter? Can you make a connection between this device and the piezoelectric disk used in the previous activities?

EXPERIMENT 8: How Can Sound Be Generated From Piezoelectricity?

Materials ● Piezoelectric disk, stereo speaker plug, electric wire cutter, soldering iron, solder, tape recorder or stereo receiver

Procedure ●

1. Prepare a piezoelectric disk with soldered wire leads (see Experiment 5). If you used the same disk you constructed in the earlier activity you need to remove the Ne2 neon bulb.
2. Take an ordinary stereo speaker plug and carefully strip off about 2.5 cm of insulation. You will find two types of wires beneath the outer insulation. One type is a thin insulated wire and the other is several strands of thin, bare wire.
3. Solder the leads from the piezoelectric disk to the leads of the stereo plug.
4. Plug the stereo plug into the tape recorder or stereo receiver. Turn on the recorder or receiver. What happens to the disk? Can you see or hear any vibration?
5. Put the disk flat against the desktop or window. How does this affect what you saw or heard earlier?

Time to think ●

How do you explain what you saw/heard by applying the "reverse piezoelectric theory"? What happened when electricity from the tape recorder was applied to the piezoelectric disk?

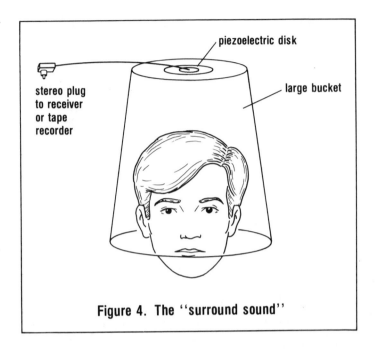

piezoelectric disk

stereo plug
to receiver
or tape
recorder

large bucket

Figure 4. The "surround sound"

EXPERIMENT 9: How Can an Inexpensive "Surround Sound" Be Made?

Materials ● All the materials used in Experiment 8 plus adhesive tape, cardboard bucket like those used in fast-food restaurants for fried chicken (large enough to fit your head)

Procedure ● (see Figure 4)

1. Prepare the piezoelectric disk, the stereo plug, and the tape recorder or stereo receiver as you did in Experiment 8. Follow steps 1 through 4 of that experiment.

2. Tape the piezoelectric disk flat to the bottom of the bucket.

3. Place your head inside the bucket and turn on the tape recorder or stereo receiver. Can you describe what happens?

Time to Think ●

- How was the quality of "surround sound" different from the sound production of Experiment 8?
- How did the bucket act as a chamber of resonance?
- Based on what you learned from this activity, can you hypothesize how microchips are similarly used in buzzers and watch tones?

3

ELECTRICITY
IN MOTION

When you turn on an electric appliance, the electricity that makes it go is not magically produced at the wall socket. Electricity has to be generated from an energy source such as a power station generator or a battery (which basically is a portable power station). The electricity is then delivered to the consumer through cables. The cable is like a water main between the reservoir and your home.

In order for our homes to receive electric power, there has to be a power station to generate the power and a cable to deliver it. In other words, both the source and the pathway are needed to convey the moving electricity. If either the station generators stop working or the cable is broken, electricity stops running.

Put simply, electricity is a form of energy that makes things go and glow, a form of energy that can be changed into mechanical, light, or heat energy. A great deal of the moving electricity used in the home is changed into heat energy. The flowing electrons are used to heat the elements in an electric range, a toaster, or a heating system.

Electrical energy also may be converted to light energy in a light bulb, or to sound energy in a radio or a television speaker. Electric current can also produce mechanical energy, which can be used to turn motors in a dishwasher, washing machine, or electric blender.

HISTORY

Alessandro Volta ● The Italian physicist Alessandro Volta (1745–1827) invented a device called the electrophorus, which used metal plates to store electric charge. The stored electricity could be drained and used. This could be considered the primitive model of today's electric battery and condenser. Count Volta, a nobleman, established an important theory of current electricity, which deals with the movement of electrons. The theory states that electrons move from a location of high energy to a location of low energy by virtue of their relative position in the electric field. The term *electric potential* is used to describe the energy level of electrons. The unit of electric potential is the volt, named after Volta.

Volta invented his "voltaic piles," a forerunner of the modern battery, in 1799. It consists of alternating disks of copper and zinc, with salt-water-saturated pads layered between them. Volta is credited with the discovery of constant-current electricity.

Georg Simon Ohm (1787–1854) demonstrated that flow of current is directly proportional to difference in electric potential and inversely proportional to the resistance of the conductor. This became known as Ohm's law.

Georg Simon Ohm ● Georg Simon Ohm (1787–1854), a German scientist devoted to the study of electricity, discovered that the flow of electricity is not only related to the electric potential as stated by Volta, but also to the resistance of the conducting pathway. Ohm tested the hypothesis by passing current through conductors of different length and thickness. He discovered that for a given type of metal, the flow of electricity increased as the metal's length and thickness decreased. In other words, electricity tends to seek a pathway with the least resistance.

BACKGROUND INFORMATION

Earlier we said that the electricity we use every day requires both an electric source and an electric pathway. What we were talking about, in effect, was the electric circuit—the source and pathway put together. The electric circuit is a continuous path through which electric charges flow, and the flow is called an electric current. Electricity must travel in a complete circuit in order to be used.

Conventionally, we use electron flow to describe the movement of current. The amount of current is measured in terms of a unit called the ampere, or amp. The ampere unit measures the quantity of charges that passes by a point in a given time. For example, a typical household light bulb (100 watt) uses 1 ampere of electricity.

Every circuit must of course have a source of energy supply, which can be a battery or a generator. In a battery, current is generated by stored chemical energy. Because the current always flows in one direction, it is called direct current (DC). Current flow from a generator, on the other hand, changes, or alternates, in direction and is therefore called alternating current (AC).

EXPERIMENT 10: How Much Electricity Do You Use?

Materials • None needed

Procedure • (see Figure 5)

1. Locate the electric meter in your house or apartment, which measures kilowatt-hours. Look at it carefully. It will be either the new-style digital display or the old-style dial meter. Both types of meters will change their number as electricity is being used in your home.
2. If you have the dial meter, note that the dials are organized to be read in multiples of 10. The dial farthest to the right indicates kilowatt-hours in 1's, the next dial in 10's, the next dial in 100's, then 1,000's, then 10,000's.
3. Read the dial of your dial meter from left to right, just as you would numbers. It can be tricky because some of the dials read clockwise, others read counterclockwise. The main thing to remember when reading a dial-type electric meter is that when the pointer is between two numbers, it is always read as the smaller number. If the pointer is exactly on the number, read it as the number. If it is only half a millimeter in front of a number, read it as the smaller number. Note that if the pointer is between 9 and 0, consider 9 to be smaller than

38

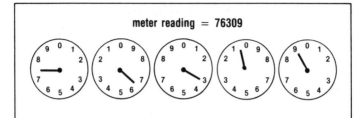

meter reading = 76309

Figure 5. How much electricity do you use?

0. The 0 is really a 10 in this case. If the pointer is between 0 and 1, read the number as 1.

4.   For either type of meter, look to find the wheel that turns when electricity is being used in the house. Ask an adult to turn on some electric appliances and watch the turning wheel of the meter.

5.   Look at the meter about the same time every day. Record the reading for several days. Find out how much electricity your house uses on average each day.

Time to Think ●

● Did your home use roughly the same amount of electricity every day? Were some days more expensive than others? If so, can you think of several reasons why?

● The turning meter wheel indicates that electricity is being used. Which appliances use the most electricity? Is it the microwave oven, the blender, the radio, the television, or the vacuum cleaner?

EXPERIMENT 11: How Many Ways Can You Light a Bulb?

Materials ● Aluminum foil, scissors, flashlight bulb, 1.5-volt dry cell (D cell) (*Note:* technically, a single dry cell should not be called a battery because a battery is two or more electric cells connected together.)

Procedure ●

1.   Cut a strip of aluminum foil about 1/2 cm wide.
2.   Construct a complete circuit using the dry cell as the energy source, the foil strip as the pathway, and the flashlight bulb as the energy user. Does the bulb light up?
3.   Record all your attempts with simple diagrams. You may use the foil strip to connect the different parts of the light bulb to the different parts of the cell. How many different ways can you light a bulb?

Time to Think ● Examine all the circuit diagrams that you have recorded. Divide them into two groups, the successful circuits (those that light the bulb) and the unsuccessful circuits. What is one major difference between the two groups?

EXPERIMENT 12: How Do You Build a Copper-Zinc Plate Battery?

Note: In 1880, Alessandro Volta (see "History," above) invented a primitive device for producing electricity by chemical reaction. Today, simple chemical cells are called voltaic cells in his honor.

Materials ● Copper strip, zinc strip, two insulated wires, crystals of ammonium chloride (sal ammoniac), thin strip of felt, hammer, scissors, rubber band, sandpaper, ruler, sheet cutter, nail, safety glasses, lab apron

Procedure ●

1. Use the sandpaper to thoroughly clean both sides of the zinc and copper strips.
2. Use the sheet cutter to cut the zinc strip into six 2-cm squares (**caution!**). Cut the copper strip likewise to obtain six 2-cm squares. Flatten the squares by hammering them on a hard surface.
3. Use scissors to cut six squares of felt smaller than the 2-cm squares.
4. Put on safety glasses and lab apron. Dissolve the ammonium chloride in a few teaspoons of warm water in a bowl. The ammonium chloride solution is the liquid conductor of the battery. **Handle the chemical solution with care**.
5. Thoroughly soak the felt squares in the ammonium chloride solution. Press the soaked felt slightly to get rid of the excess solution.
6. Place a zinc square flat on a table and cover it with a wet felt square. Then put a copper square on top of the felt square. In other words, the piece of felt is sandwiched between the zinc and copper squares. Repeat the arrangement to form a single multilayered "sandwich" as follows.

Z/F/C/Z/F/C/Z/F/C/Z/F/C/Z/F/C/Z/F/C
Zinc = Z Felt = F Copper = C

7. Use a nail and hammer to make a small hole on the first zinc square and the last copper square.

8. Tie the stack together with a rubber band. Now you have made a zinc-copper plate battery. Now complete steps 9 and 10 to find out if it will work.

9. Strip the end of an insulated wire to expose the metal. Connect the wire to the zinc square that has the hole. Similarly attach another wire to the copper square with a hole. Wash your hands clean of the chemical solution.

10. Touch your tongue with the two wires. How does it feel? Can you feel the mild electric current?

Time to Think ●

● How does the battery generate electricity?
● What would happen if just zinc or just copper squares were used?
● Is the electricity generated by your homemade battery strong enough to light a flashlight bulb? How do you find out?

EXPERIMENT 13: What Is Inside a Dry Cell?

Materials ● D cell, hacksaw, insulated wire with exposed ends, flashlight bulb, work gloves, safety glasses

Procedure ●

1. Examine the outside of the D cell. Hypothesize what the inside of the cell would look like if it were cut in half lengthwise. Illustrate your hypothesis with a simple diagram.

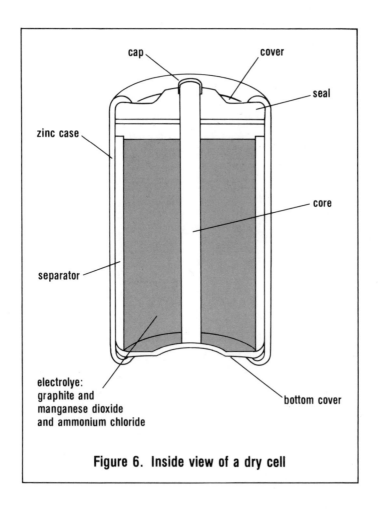

cap

cover

seal

zinc case

core

separator

electrolye:
graphite and
manganese dioxide
and ammonium chloride

bottom cover

Figure 6. Inside view of a dry cell

2.   Put on work gloves, safety glasses, and a lab apron. Cut open the cell the long way with a hacksaw. Position the saw so that it is off the center contact point. Can you identify the following parts: carbon rod, black carbon electrolyte paste made of manganese dioxide and graphite powder, and the zinc can (see Figure 6)? How does the real interior compare with your hypothesis?

(*Note:* Hold on to your cut-open cell. You can use it again for Experiment 14.)

3. Test the cell with the flashlight bulb and wire, much as you did with the bulb and foil in Experiment 11. Does the cell still produce electricity? How can you tell?

Time to Think ●

● The function of the zinc container is to produce electrons and the black electrolyte receives them. Draw a complete circuit diagram to show the flow of electrons when you connect a bulb and a wire to a cell. How does that flow of electrons explain why the bulb lights up?

● Was the inside of the cell you cut open moist or dry? Do you know why?

● Dry cells have a limited shelf life. Expired cells usually develop leaks through the cell container. Do you know why?

EXPERIMENT 14: How Do You Recycle Dry-Cell Parts to Make a Wet Cell?

Materials ● D cell, insulated wires with exposed ends, flashlight bulb, hacksaw, salt, glass jar, nail and hammer

Procedure ● (see Figure 7)

1. If you saved the cell you cut open in Experiment 13, go right on to step 2. Otherwise, put on work gloves

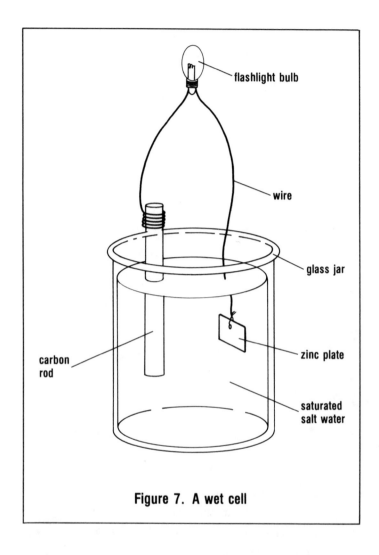

Figure 7. A wet cell

and safety glasses and cut open the D cell lengthwise with a hacksaw.

2. Remove the carbon rod in the center and clean it.
3. Cut a strip of the zinc can (this is the shell or

45

container of the cell) about the length and width of the carbon rod. Clean the strip well.

4.   Using a nail, hammer a small hole on one end of the zinc strip. Attach a wire to the zinc through the hole. Loop another wire around the rod to attach it. Make sure that the ends of the wires are stripped to expose the metal.

5.   Lower the carbon rod and the piece of zinc into a glass jar of saturated salt water (water with a lot of dissolved salt). Make sure that the wires hang outside the jar. Now you have completed the construction of a wet cell. Why is it called a wet cell?

6.   Connect the wires to a flashlight bulb. Did you build a complete circuit to produce electricity? How can you tell?

7.   Draw a diagram of your hookup to show the direction of electron flow through the wet-cell system.

Time to Think ●

● What is the major structural difference between a dry cell and a wet cell? Which parts are comparable and which are not?

● Are the contact points on the wet cell similar to the contact points on the dry cell? Can you explain?

● Can you explain the flow of electrons in the wet cell with reference to the electric potential of the zinc and the carbon? Which one has a higher electric potential? The electrons always flow from a point of higher electric potential to one of lower potential.

● Insert a carbon rod and a piece of zinc from a used

46

dry cell into a fresh lemon. Using insulated wires, connect the rod and the zinc to a flashlight bulb to make a complete circuit. The bulb lights up. How do you explain what you saw?

EXPERIMENT 15: What Is Inside a Light Bulb?

Materials ● Frosted household light bulb, hacksaw, work gloves, cloth rag, hammer, safety glasses, pliers

Procedure ●

1.   Examine the frosted household light bulb to identify the glass and the metal base. What do you think the inside of the bulb would be like if you were able to see through the frosted glass and the metal base? Draw a diagram of your hypothesis.

2.   Wear your safety glasses to protect your eyes. Wrap the bulb completely with a cloth rag and hammer lightly enough to break only the glass and not the parts inside the bulb.

Now, what do you see? Can you find the coiled filament and the glass support? Why are the two ends of the filament separated by glass?

3.   Cut open the metal base of the bulb carefully with the hacksaw. Remove the metal covering with pliers. Wear your work gloves to protect your hands from sharp edges. What is inside? Can you trace the ends of the filament through the metal base? Where are the wire contacts inside the metal base?

4.   Draw a diagram showing the inside of the entire light bulb. How is this diagram different from the one

you hypothesized earlier? In your notebook, write how you think a light bulb works.

Time to Think ●

- Why are the metal base and the wire contact points of a light bulb separated by ceramic material?
- In order to light up a bulb, a complete electric circuit has to be established. Based on what you see inside the bulb, which two specific contact points should the wire touch to light up the bulb?

EXPERIMENT 16: How Do You Build a Cell Holder, a Bulb Holder and a Switch?

Materials ● D cell, masking tape, two large paper clips, two wood boards (5 × 6 × 1 cm), clothespin, thumbtacks, noninsulated copper wire, ruler with a shallow channel in the middle, flashlight bulb

Procedure ● (see Figure 8)

Dry-Cell Holder ○

1. Place the two large clips against the two ends of the D cell. Make sure that the clip touches the end contact of the cell. The loop end of the clip should extend beyond the diameter of the cell. With the clips in position, secure them by wrapping masking tape around the cell lengthwise. Place the cell on the shallow channel of the ruler; the channel will hold the cell in place and prevent it from rolling. Now you have assembled a dry

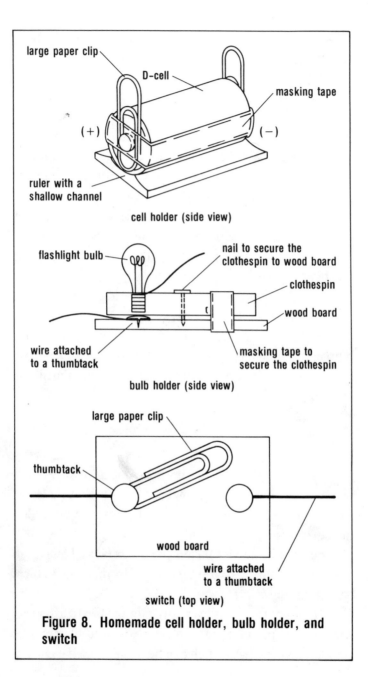

Figure 8. Homemade cell holder, bulb holder, and switch

cell with two terminal attachments resting on a holder (Figure 8).

Bulb Holder ○

2. Push a thumbtack gently into one end of one of the wood boards. Wrap a wire under the tack and allow a length of the wire to hang from it. Carefully hammer the tack into the board after the wire is in place.

3. Use a clothespin to hold a flashlight bulb. Place the metal base of the bulb right above the tack. Secure the clothespin and bulb by putting the clothespin flat on the board. Drive a small nail through the hole in the middle of the clothespin and use masking tape to attach the clothespin to the wood block.

4. Wrap another wire around the metal base of the bulb and extend a length of the wire from the bulb. Now you have made yourself a bulb holder with a flashlight bulb in place.

Switch ○

5. Push two thumbtacks into the opposite sides of a wood board. Wrap a wire under one tack. Place a large paper clip and the end of another length of wire under the second tack. You should make sure that when the paper clip is turned it touches the other tack. The paper clip is the bridge between the two tacks that acts to turn the circuit on or off.

6. Hammer the tacks carefully into the board after the wires and paper clip are in place. Now you have made yourself a switch. A switch can be used to open a circuit

(make it an incomplete circuit) or to close it (make it complete).

Time to Think ● What is the key factor to consider in putting the bulb, the dry cell, and the switch together to make a complete circuit?

EXPERIMENT 17: How Can You Make a Circuit Using a Switch, a Bulb and a Cell?

Materials ● D cell with holder, flashlight bulb with holder, and switch—all from Experiment 16

Procedure ●

1. Connect the D cell with its holder, the flashlight bulb with its holder, and the switch to make a circuit. (*Hint:* connect the paper clip of the D cell to one end of the wire of the bulb holder. Connect the second end of the wire from the bulb holder to one wire of the switch. Connect the second wire from the switch to the other clip of the D cell.) Do you now have a complete circuit? Can you explain?
2. Turn the paper clip to bridge the two thumbtacks. Do you have an open or closed circuit? How can you tell? How can you turn the light on and off by using only the switch?

Time to Think ● In a simple circuit the cell is the energy source and the bulb is the energy user. Will an open switch make the circuit complete or incomplete? What then is the function of the switch?

EXPERIMENT 18: How Do You Test Conductors and Insulators?

Materials ● Flashlight bulb, D cell, wire, paper clip, eraser, chalk, pencil lead, paper, glass

Procedure ● (see Figure 9)

1. Construct a complete electric circuit using the cell, the wire, and the light bulb. If you have completed Experiment 17 this should not be a new experience.
2. Place different objects between the contact points of the circuit (for example, between the bulb and the cell or between the wire and the cell). Test some other substances that you have in mind. Record the results in the following chart.

Objects	Lights the Bulb	Does Not Light the Bulb	Conductor/ Insulator
Clip	_____	_____	_____
Eraser	_____	_____	_____
Chalk	_____	_____	_____
Lead	_____	_____	_____
Paper	_____	_____	_____
Glass	_____	_____	_____
Other	_____	_____	_____

Time to Think ●

● Conductors permit electric current to flow through them while insulators do not. Can you classify the

What are the conductive properties of these materials?
You can find out by doing Experiment 18.

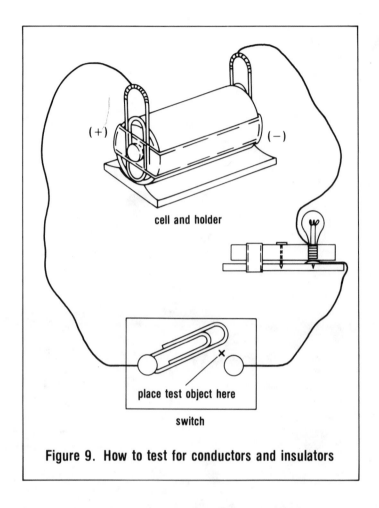

(+)   (−)

cell and holder

place test object here

switch

Figure 9. How to test for conductors and insulators

objects in this experiment into two groups: conductors and insulators?
• Can you identify the different parts of a dry cell
and a light bulb as either conductors or insulators?
Why are both conductors and insulators used in
making a dry cell and a light bulb?

EXPERIMENT 19: What Is an Electrolyte?

Materials ● D cell, three insulated wires, small glass jar, flashlight bulb, bulb socket, sugar, vinegar, salt, starch, cooking oil, water, masking tape, six small paper cups, teaspoon

Procedure ● (see Figure 10)

1.   Strip the ends of all three insulated wires.
2.   Connect one wire between one terminal attachment of the cell and the bulb socket.
3.   Connect one end of the second wire to the socket, leaving the other end free.
4.   Connect one end of the third wire to the other terminal of the cell.
5.   Place the wire from the socket and the cell into a jar as shown in the diagram.
6.   Fill one of the small paper cups with cooking oil and another with water. Use the masking tape to label the two cups "water" and "cooking oil" and set them aside. Now fill the other four cups with water. Prepare these test solutions by stirring each of the other substances—the sugar, vinegar, salt, and starch—into a separate cup until the water can dissolve no more of the substance. In any case put no more than two teaspoons of the substance into its cup. Be sure to identify what you have placed in each cup with a masking tape label right after adding the substance.
7.   Separately pour each of the six test liquids into the jar. Before adding another liquid, be sure to empty the jar and thoroughly rinse it with plain water. Whenever

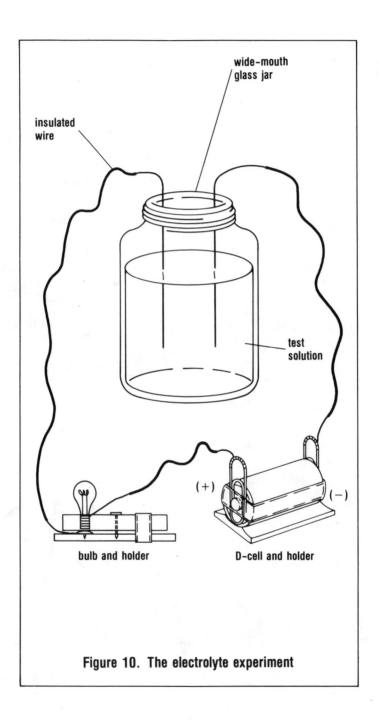

Figure 10. The electrolyte experiment

you pour a liquid into the jar, make sure the free ends of the wires are submerged. Use the following chart to record your observations.

Test Solutions	Does the Bulb Light Up? (Yes/No)
Water	
Oil	
Sugar water	
Vinegar water	
Salt water	
Starch water	

8. Look at the completed chart. Which liquid permits electricity to flow through? Liquids that permit the passage of electricity are nonmetallic conductors in which current is carried by the movement of ions. Liquid conductors are called electrolytes.

EXPERIMENT 20: What Is Electroplating?

Materials • 6-volt cell, old door key, copper strip, nail, hammer, salt and vinegar, small glass jar, insulated wire, masking tape

Procedure • (see Figure 11)

1. Fill the small glass jar about half full with vinegar. Stir in salt (about one tablespoon) until the vinegar can dissolve it no more. You will notice a small deposit of salt at the bottom of the jar when the salt-vinegar solution is ready.

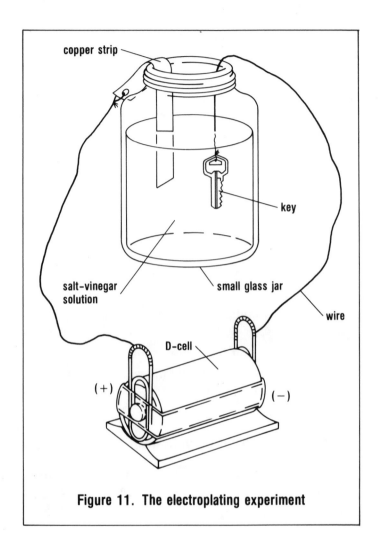

copper strip

key

salt-vinegar solution

small glass jar

wire

D-cell

(+)

(-)

Figure 11. The electroplating experiment

2. Hammer a small hole into one end of the copper strip with a nail. Bend the copper strip so that the long end is submerged in the solution while the short end with the hole hangs outside the jar.

3. Strip the ends of the insulated wire to expose the metal. Connect the wire between one terminal of the cell and the nail hole of the copper strip. Use the masking tape to secure the wire to the dry cell terminal.

4. Strip the ends of another wire to expose the metal. Connect the wire between the free terminal of the cell and the key.

5. Submerge the key in the salt-vinegar solution. Make sure that the key and the copper strip are not touching each other.

6. Wait for a few minutes and record your observations. What happened to the color of the solution? What happened to the key?

Time to Think ●

● Can you trace the path of electricity in the electroplating system by identifying all the components? (*Hint:* the source of electricity is the dry cell. Begin with the dry cell and trace the path through the wire and back to the dry cell.)
● Predict what will happen if plain water is used instead of the salt-vinegar solution.
● How does the copper deposit on the key?
● How is electroplating used in industry? Can you give examples?

EXPERIMENT 21: How Can Two Light Bulbs (in Series) Be Lit at the Same Time?

Materials ● D cell with holder, two flashlight bulbs with holders, switch, four lengths of noninsulated copper wire

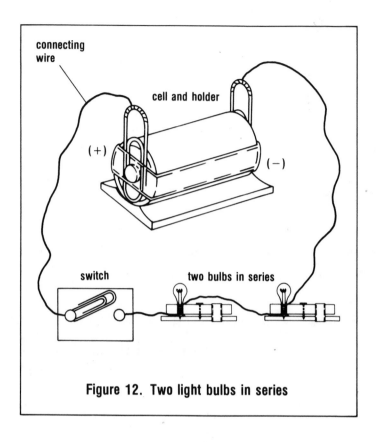

connecting
wire

cell and holder

(+)

(−)

switch

two bulbs in series

Figure 12. Two light bulbs in series

Procedure ● (see Figure 12)

1. If you skipped Experiment 16, then you will have
to go back and make the D cell holder, bulb holder, and
switch described in that experiment. You will need to
build an extra bulb holder, however. If you have already
completed Experiment 16, then of course all you have
to build is the second bulb holder.

2. Connect one wire to the terminal (that is, the paper

clip) of the cell and to one end of the switch. You may twist the wires together to secure the connections.

3. Connect a second wire from the other terminal (paper clip) of the cell to one terminal of the bulb holder.

4. Connect a third wire between the remaining terminal of the first bulb holder and one terminal of the second bulb holder.

5. Connect a fourth wire between the remaining terminal of the second bulb holder and the last terminal of the switch.

6. Now you have connected all the parts of a circuit with two light bulbs in series.

7. Close the switch. What happens?

8. Remove one light bulb from the holder with the switch closed. What happens?

Time to Think ● ·

● Draw a diagram showing the flow of electrons through the complete circuit from the energy source to the energy user. Use arrows to indicate the direction of flow.

● Compare the brightness of the light bulbs in this experiment and Experiment 17. Can you explain the difference?

EXPERIMENT 22: What Are the Effects of Connecting Two Cells (in Series) in a Circuit?

Materials ● flashlight bulb with holder, switch, two D cells with holders (you will have to build one more D cell holder), noninsulated copper wire

Procedure ● (see Figure 13)

1. Connect a wire between the terminals of cell 1 and cell 2. The remainder of the connections are similar to those in Experiment 17. Remember when two cells are connected in series, the positive terminal of one cell must be connected to the negative terminal of the other cell. The experiment will not work if the terminals of the cells are not connected right.
2. Connect one wire between the other terminal of the cell holder and one terminal of the bulb holder.
3. Connect another wire from the other bulb holder terminal to one terminal of the switch.
4. Connect the last wire from the other terminal of the switch back to the terminal of the bulb holder. Now you have built a circuit with two cells in series.
5. Close the switch and observe. What happens?

Time to Think ●

- Compare the brightness of the bulb in this experiment with the one in Experiment 17, where only one cell is used. Can you explain the difference?
- When you connect two cells together what is the total voltage?

EXPERIMENT 23: How Can Two Light Bulbs (in Parallel) Be Lit at the Same Time?

Materials ● From Experiment 21: two flashlight bulbs with holders, switch, D cell with holder, noninsulated copper wires

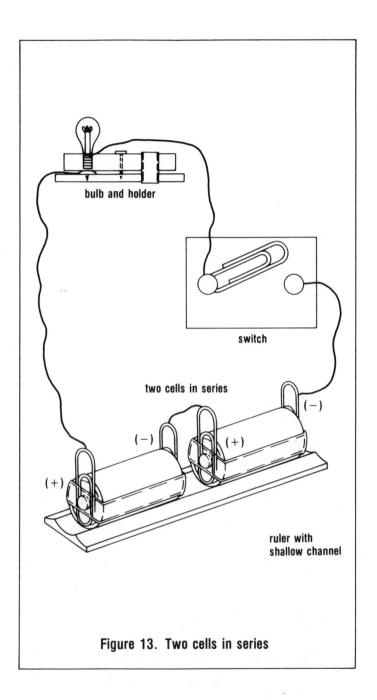

bulb and holder

switch

two cells in series

(−)

(−)

(+)

(+)

ruler with
shallow channel

Figure 13. Two cells in series

Procedure • (see Figure 14)

1. Connect one bulb and its holder, the switch, and the D cell and its holder in a complete circuit. Please see the preceding experiment for the setup.
2. Now bring in the second bulb and its holder. Connect another wire between other terminals of bulb holders 1 and 2. Notice there are two wires coming out of each terminal of bulb holder 1. Now you have completed all the parts in a circuit with two light bulbs in a parallel configuration.
3. Close the switch. What do you see?
4. Remove one light bulb from the holder with the switch closed. What happens?

Time to Think •

• Draw a diagram showing the flow of electrons through the complete circuit from the energy source to the energy user. Use arrows to indicate the direction of flow.
• Compare the brightness of the light bulbs in this experiment and Experiment 17. Can you explain?
• If you could use either a series circuit or a parallel circuit, which one would you choose and why?
• Look around your house. Can you find examples of series circuits and parallel circuits?

EXPERIMENT 24: What Are the Effects of Connecting Two Cells (in Parallel) in a Circuit?

Materials • From Experiment 16: two D cells with holders (unless you have done Experiment 22, you will

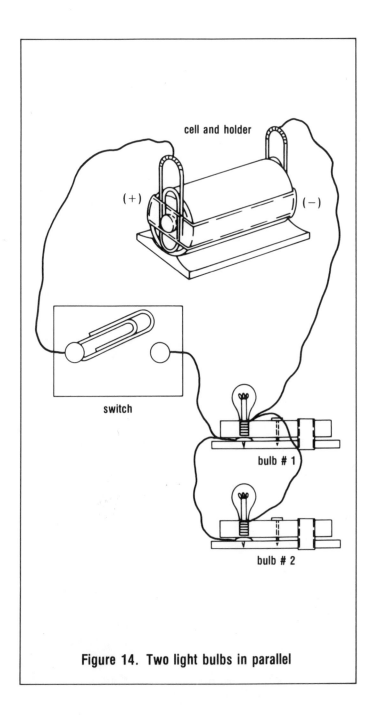

cell and holder

(+)   (−)

switch

bulb # 1

bulb # 2

Figure 14. Two light bulbs in parallel

have to build a second cell holder), flashlight bulb with holder, switch, noninsulated copper wire

Procedure ● (see Figure 15)

1.   Place the two D cells in parallel and connect the terminals with wires. Remember to place the cells so that their positive/negative terminals face the same side.
2.   Connect one wire from one terminal of cell holder 1 to the bulb holder.
3.   Connect the other terminal of the bulb holder to the switch with another wire.
4.   Make the last connection between the switch and the cell holder. Now you have completed a circuit with two cells in a parallel configuration.
5.   Close the switch and observe. What happens?

Time to Think ●

● Compare the brightness of the light bulbs in this experiment and Experiment 22, when two cells were used in series. Can you explain the difference?
● Now that you have seen a circuit with cells in series and another with cells in parallel, which one do you think is more useful or functional? Can you support your choice?

EXPERIMENT 25: How Can Electricity Be Regulated by a Rheostat?

Materials ● Flashlight bulb with holder and D cell with holder (both from Experiment 16), soft lead pencil, two iron nails, sharp knife, insulated wire, ruler

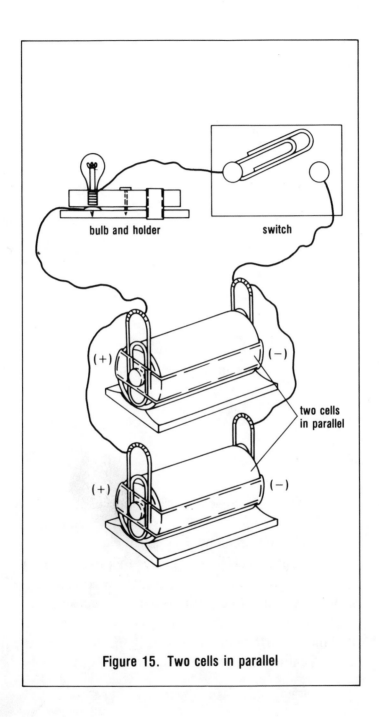

bulb and holder

switch

(+)   (−)

(+)   (−)

two cells
in parallel

Figure 15. Two cells in parallel

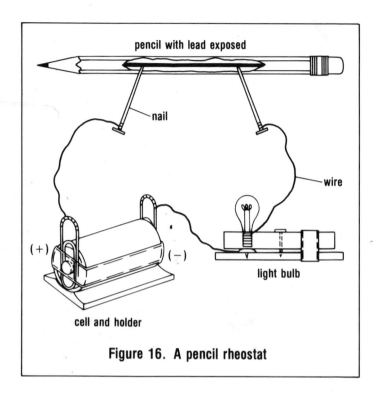

pencil with lead exposed

nail

wire

(+)   (−)

light bulb

cell and holder

Figure 16. A pencil rheostat

Procedure ● (see Figure 16)

1. Construct a simple electric circuit using the cell holder, the bulb holder, and wires as in Experiment 17.
2. Modify the circuit by wrapping the wire ends from the bulb holder and the cell holder tightly around the heads of the iron nails. The nails will be used as probes.
3. Have an adult help you to carefully cut open the soft lead pencil lengthwise with the sharp knife to expose the lead. Be careful not to break the lead. You will need its entire length for this experiment.

4. With all the circuit components in place, press the two probes (that is, nails) gently against the pencil lead. If you press too hard you will break the lead. Note that the probes should not be touching each other. What happened to the light bulb?

5. Vary the distance between the two probes along the lead and record your observations using the following table.

Distance Between the Probes (in millimeters)	Brightness of Bulb
1	
2	
3	
4	
5	
6	
7	
8	
9	
10	

Time to Think ●

- The "lead" of a pencil is mostly graphite. Is graphite a good conductor of electricity? How can you find out?
- According to the experiment data collected, how does the length of the lead affect the amount of electric current that flows through a circuit?

69

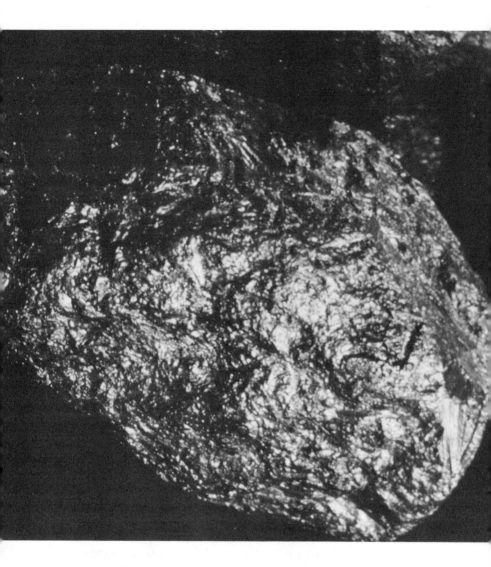

Graphite is a form of carbon. A pencil "lead" is actually mostly graphite. What do you learn about graphite's ability to regulate electric flow by making the rheostat in Experiment 25?

- A rheostat is a device for controlling the flow of electricity. For example, ordinary room lights can be dimmed by a rheostat. The volume of a radio can also be controlled by a rheostat, although nowadays electronic circuitry is used instead. How was the pencil lead used to control electrical flow? What is the major variable used in a rheostat to control the flow of electricity? Is it the length of the substance? Its weight? Its volume? What did you learn from the experiment?

EXPERIMENT 26: How Does a Two-Way Switch Work in a Circuit?

Materials • Bulb with holder and D cell with holder (from Experiment 16), two two-way switches, noninsulated copper wires

Procedure • (see Figure 17)

1. Use the diagram to prepare two two-way switches. Please note that a regular switch has only one contact, which is represented by the metal tack. The two-way switch has two contacts, or two tacks.
2. Use Figure 17 to build an incomplete circuit. In this circuit, the battery holder is connected to the bulb holder and one two-way switch. The other terminal of the bulb holder is connected to the second two-way switch.
3. How do you connect both two-way switches to make a complete circuit? (*Hint:* two wires are needed for the connection.)

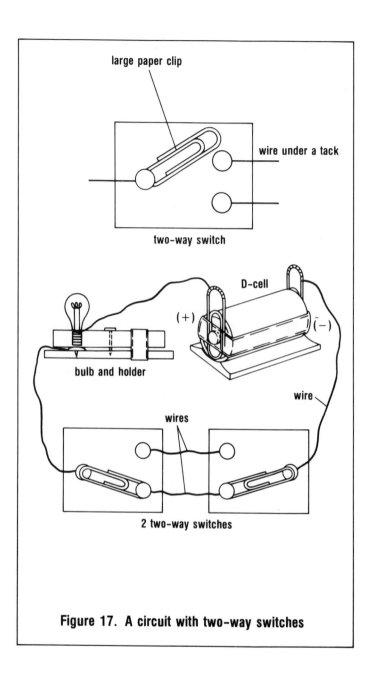

Figure 17. A circuit with two-way switches

4. Close the two switches. Does the bulb light up? Open either of the switches. What happens? Can you explain with a simple circuit diagram?

Time to Think ●

● Why would anyone want to have two switches to turn the same light on or off? What is one major advantage of having two switches?
● Why is the special switch called a two-way?

EXPERIMENT 27: How Does a Fuse Work in a Circuit?

Materials ●

6-volt cell, wooden board (5 × 6 × 1 cm), aluminum foil, scissors, noninsulated copper wires, masking tape, iron nail

Procedure ●

1. Cut a strip of aluminum foil so that the center is as thin as a wire. The thickness of the wire is critical to the success of the experiment. This prepared strip is called a fuse.
2. Place the fuse flat on the wood board and connect each end with a wire. The connections between the wire and the fuse can be secured by masking tape.
3. Connect the wire to the two terminals of the 6-volt cell.
4. Observe what happens and record your observations.

Time to Think •

• Can you locate a fuse box (circuit breaker box) in your house? How is the fuse box similar to the fuse in the experiment?
• Can you explain how a fuse protects an overloaded electric circuit? Please keep in mind that most wiring systems today use circuit breakers instead of fuses.

EXPERIMENT 28: What is a Circuit Resistance?

Materials • Thin insulated wires, thick insulated wires, thumbtacks, two wooden boards (5 × 15 cm), flashlight bulb with holder, D cell with holder, switch

Procedure • (see Figure 18)

1. Use the flashlight bulb and holder, the D cell and holder, and the switch to build a simple electric circuit like the one in Experiment 17. Use thin wires for all connections.
2. Use an extra-long piece of wire between the bulb holder and the cell holder. Wrap the wire around a piece of board, and secure it with two thumbtacks hammered into the board.
3. Close the switch, and record what you observe.
4. Disconnect the wires and replace them with thick wires. Again, use an extra-long piece of thick wire (about the same length as the extra-long thin wire) between the bulb holder and the cell holder. As before,

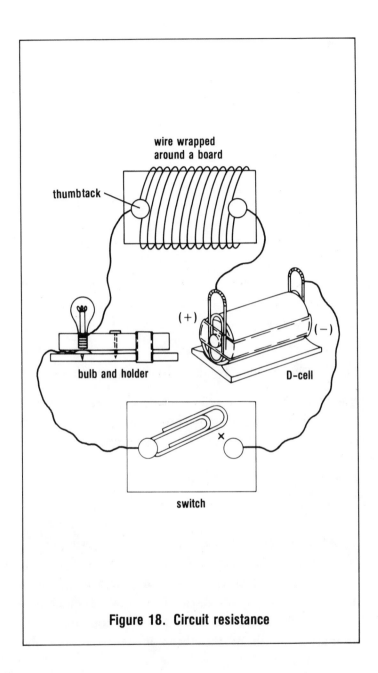

wire wrapped
around a board

thumbtack

(+)

(−)

bulb and holder

D-cell

×

switch

Figure 18. Circuit resistance

wrap this wire around a piece of board and secure it with two thumbtacks.

5. Close the switch and record your observations.

Time to Think ●

- How does length affect the electrical resistance in a wire?
- How does thickness affect the electrical resistance in a wire?
- Does electrical resistance affect the brightness of a light bulb?
- Which component—the light bulb, the D cell, or the switch—offers the most resistance to the flow of electrons? Can you support your answer?

EXPERIMENT 29: How Is Electricity Changed to Heat?

Materials ● D cell with holder, switch, nichrome heating wire (from a science supply store or an electronic store), connecting wire, thermometer, graph paper

Procedure ● (See Figure 19)

1. Use the D cell with holder, and the switch, to build a simple electric circuit like the one in Experiment 17. Note that instead of a flashlight bulb and holder, you will be connecting a special nichrome heating wire between a terminal of the switch and a terminal of the cell holder.

2. Coil the nichrome wire tightly about ten turns around the bulb of the thermometer (Caution! the nichrome wire will get hot!)

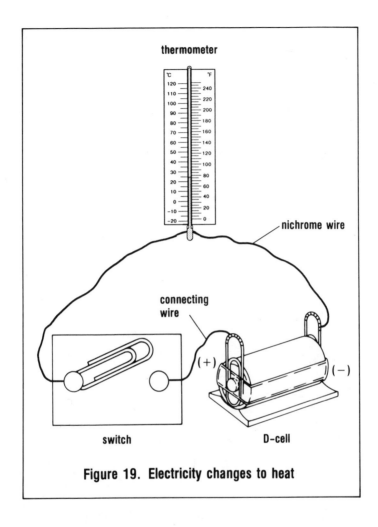

thermometer

nichrome wire

connecting wire

switch

D-cell

Figure 19. Electricity changes to heat

3.   Record the beginning temperature of the thermom-eter. To avoid affecting the accuracy of the temperature reading, be careful not to touch the glass stem or the thermometer bulb.

4.   Close the switch and read the thermometer at 15-

second intervals. Use the following table to record your observations.

Time (seconds)	Temperature (degrees Celsius)
Start	
15	
30	
45	
60	
75	
90	
105	
120	
135	
150	
165	
180	
195	

5. Use the data you collected to construct a line graph. Place the time variable (seconds) on the X axis and the temperature variable (degrees Celsius) on the Y axis.

Time to Think ●

● The nichrome heating wire has very high resistance to the flow of electricity. How is this property related to changing electricity to heat?

● Can you name a few household examples where electricity is turned into heat?

● A heating element is an object made of a high-resistance substance like nichrome which is tightly coiled to concentrate the heat produced. If you were an electrical technician, how would you design the heating element for an electric coffeepot?

- Examine the contour of the line graph from the experiment. What is the maximum temperature? What is the difference between the maximum temperature and the beginning temperature?

EXPERIMENT 30: How Is Electricity Changed to Light?

Materials • Two D cells with holders, three wires, switch, nichrome wire, ruler

Procedure •

1. Connect the two cell holders and cells with a length of wire. Add the switch to the circuit you are building.
2. Wrap the length of nichrome wire around the ends of the two wires coming from the incomplete circuit.
3. Close the switch. What happens? (*Caution:* the nichrome wire gets very hot!)
4. Vary the length of the nichrome wire connection and complete the following table.

Length of the Nichrome Wire	Brightness of the Wire
5 mm	
10 mm	
15 mm	
20 mm	

5. How does the length of the nichrome wire connection affect the brightness of the wire?

Time to Think ● Based on your experience of the experiment, can you explain how electricity is changed to light energy?

EXPERIMENT 31: How Does a Diode Work?

A diode is a semiconductor device that permits electric current to flow in one direction. A diode is like a one-way street for electricity. It is one of many devices used by engineers to make televisions, radios, and other electronic appliances.

Materials ● D cell with holder, flashlight bulb with holder, long piece of wire, switch, simple diode (from an electronics store)

Procedure ● (see Figure 20)

1. Connect the D-cell, the light bulb, and the switch to make a complete circuit similar to the one in Experiment 17.
2. Now connect the diode to the circuit as shown in Figure 20. What happens to the light?
3. Now turn the diode around 180 degrees so that the connecting wires are attached to the opposite ends of the diode wires. What happens to the light now?

Time to Think ● How would you define *diode*? Write your definition in your notebook.

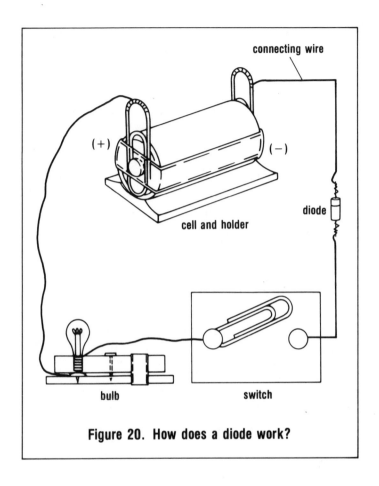

connecting wire

(+)

(−)

diode

cell and holder

bulb

switch

Figure 20. How does a diode work?

EXPERIMENT 32: How Do You Wire a "House"?

Now that you have worked with different circuits in this chapter, you can try to wire a shoe box in the same way that an electrician wires a house.

Materials ● Shoe box, cardboard, scissors, pencil, ruler,

wires, four flashlight bulbs, switch, D cell with holder, masking tape

Procedure ●

1. Cut up the cardboard and use the pieces as dividers to make four rooms in the shoe box "house."

2. Draw a plan for placing a light in each of the four rooms. Consider the following questions: Where will the light be placed? Where will the switch be placed? Where will the electrical source be placed? How will you connect everything to make a complete circuit?

3. Go ahead with the wiring after you have completed the wiring plan in your notebook. Turn on the switch. Does your wiring plan work? If it doesn't, try a different plan.

Time to Think ● How should the switch, bulbs, and cells be connected so that the lights in the house are the brightest possible?

4

ELECTROMAGNETISM

What do doorbells, television sets, vacuum cleaners, hair dryers, fans, electric razors, electric can openers, washing machines, telegraphs, telephones, electric motors, and generators have in common? They all use electromagnets activated by the flow of electricity. Electromagnetism works wonders in our daily lives, as you can see from the roll call of household gadgets and appliances that use electromagnetism to do their jobs. In the following experiments you will experience firsthand the close relationship between magnetism and electricity.

HISTORY

Hans Christian Oersted • In 1820 the Danish physicist Hans Christian Oersted (1777–1851) discovered the close relationship between electricity and magnetism. The story of the discovery is an interesting one. While giving a college physics lecture, he noticed that a nearby compass needle twitched when he flipped a switch to start an electric current. Further experiments convinced him that a magnetic field is present whenever electric current flows through a wire.

André-Marie Ampère • The French physicist and mathematician André-Marie Ampère (1775–1836) repeated Oersted's experiment many times to define a rule. The rule relates the direction of current electricity along a wire to the deflection of the compass needle. Ampere then proposed a theory of magnetism that explained it in terms of the flow of an electric current. The theory reflected his conviction that electric current causes the phenomenon of electro/magnetism.

In recognition of Ampere's contribution to the understanding of electromagnetism, the unit of electric current was named after him. An ampere of electricity is defined as the amount of current in a wire that will exert a certain force on another nearby current-carrying wire.

Background information • Electricity and magnetism are inseparable aspects of the same phenomenon: you cannot have one without the other. Simply stated, wherever there is a moving electric field, a magnetic force may

Danish physicist Hans Christian Oersted (1777–1851) demonstrated the effect of an electric current on a magnetic compass needle. His discovery became the foundation of the study of electromagnetism.

be induced in a nearby conductor. On the other hand, wherever there is a moving electric current, there is a magnetic field.

One common application of electromagnetism is the electromagnet, a device used in such machines as the telegraph, the buzzer, and the motor, among other gadgets and appliances. A simple electromagnet is a loop of wire coiled around an iron core and connected to the two terminals of a battery. Due to the connection between magnetism and electricity, the current produces a magnetic field; therefore the loop of wire acts as a magnet. The strength of the electromagnet can be augmented by increasing the number of coil turns or by boosting the electrical input from the source. Unlike the permanent magnets that you use to hold things on your refrigerator, the electromagnet can be turned on and off by opening and closing the switch that controls the current.

The other side of the electromagnetic coin relates to the ability of the magnetic field to produce electricity. If the magnetic field in the region of a loop of wire is changed by moving a bar magnet near the wire, electrons will flow in the wire. Why? Because the magnetic field pushes the electrons, and moving electrons produce electricity. This phenomenon is called electromagnetic induction.

EXPERIMENT 33: How Do You Make a Galvanometer (Electric Current Detector)?

Materials ● 6-volt dry cell, various lengths of insulated wire, magnetic compass, cover of a small cardboard box, four thumbtacks, switch (from Experiment 16), wooden board, two paper clips

Procedure ● (see Figure 21)

1.   Coil an insulated wire about fifteen turns around the cover of a small cardboard box.

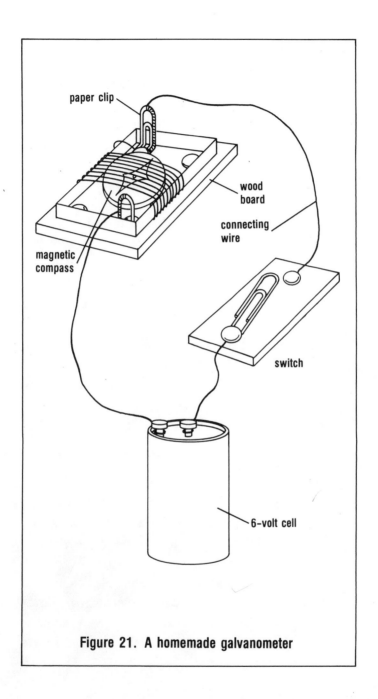

Figure 21. A homemade galvanometer

2. Place the box cover on the board. Secure it in place at the corners with four thumbtacks.

3. Bend two paper clips in half as shown. The paper clips are the leads.

4. Slip the paper clips under the tacks. Wrap the ends of the wire around the thumbtacks. Press the tacks into the wood.

5. Put the magnetic compass inside the box, that is, inside the wire coil.

6. Connect a wire between the cell terminal and the switch terminal.

7. Connect two other wires from the cell and switch to the paper clip leads.

8. Close the switch. What happens? Open and close the switch several times and record your observations.

9. Reconnect the terminals of the cell to reverse the poles. In other words, the wire used to connect the positive end now connects the negative end and vice versa. Close the switch. What happens? Open and close the switch several times and record your observations.

Time to Think •

- Based on the results of the experiment, can you formulate a simple rule to describe the relationship between the direction of the current and the movement of the compass needle?

- Consider the close link between electricity and magnetism—that is, when electricity moves through a coil, magnetism is produced. Explain how a galvanometer is used to detect electric current.

EXPERIMENT 34: How Do You Make a Simple Electromagnet?

Materials • 6-volt cell, insulated bell wire, large iron nail, switch (from Experiment 16), straight pins

Procedure •

1. Coil an insulated wire twenty turns around a large iron nail.
2. Connect one end of the wire to the switch and the other end to the terminal of the 6-volt cell.
3. Connect a wire between the switch and the cell to make a circuit.
4. Close the switch to make a complete circuit. How many straight pins can the electromagnet you have just made pick up? Record your observation in the chart.
5. Increase the number of turns around the nail to forty, sixty, eighty, etc., according to the chart. Each time test the electromagnet on the straight pins. Record your observations in the chart.

Number of Coils	Number of Pins Picked Up
20	
40	
60	
80	
100	
120	
140	
160	
180	

Time to Think ●

● What happened to the strength of your electromagnet whenever you opened the switch? Does
this suggest any advantages of using an electromagnet?
● Use the data from the chart to plot a line graph. Use
the axis for the number of coils and the X axis for
the number of pins picked up. What does the graph
look like? What does it mean? What can you gener-
alize about the number of coils versus the strength
of the electromagnet?
● Can you imagine how a junkyard operator would
use a powerful electromagnet to move metal
scraps?

EXPERIMENT 35: How Can You Make a Stronger Electro-magnet?

Materials ● Two 6-volt cells, insulated bell wire, large
iron nail, switch (from Experiment 16), straight pins

Procedure ●

1. Construct a twenty-turn electromagnet as you first
did in Experiment 34.
2. Place two 6-volt cells in series.
3. Secure all wire connections to make a complete
circuit.
4. Close the switch. What happens? Open and close
the switch several times and record your observations.
5. Increase the number of coils around the nail to

forty, sixty, eighty, etc., according to the chart. How many pins can each electromagnet pick up? Record your observations in the chart.

Number of Coils	Number of Pins Picked Up
20	
40	
60	
80	
100	
120	
160	
180	

Time to Think ●

- Use the data from the chart to plot a line graph. Use the Y axis for the number of coils and the X axis for the number of pins picked up. What does the graph look like? What does it mean?
- Compare the graph to the graph in Experiment 34. What generalization can you make about how to strengthen an electromagnet?
- How would you design an electromagnetic device to detect counterfeit coins?

EXPERIMENT 36: How Do You Build a Telegraph Set?

Materials ● 6-volt cell, wood block, two large iron nails, switch, pieces of unpainted ferrous metal such as iron, nickel, steel, noninsulated bell wire, screw, hammer

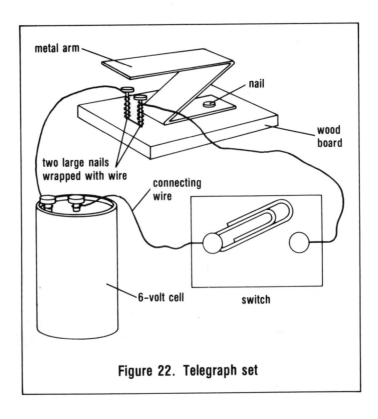

Figure 22. Telegraph set

Procedure ● (see Figure 22)

1. Bend a piece of metal into a Z-shape and nail it on the block of wood as shown. This piece of metal is the receiver of the telegraph set.

2. Hammer the two iron nails under the free end of the metal.

3. Connect a long piece of wire to one terminal of the 6-volt cell.

4. Wrap the wire many times around the nail until the

nail is covered with layers of coil. Start at the top of the nail and work downward.

5. Bring the wire across to the other nail. Coil it around as many times as before, but this time work upward.

6. Connect the other end of this wire to one terminal of the switch.

7. Connect a second wire between the free terminal of the dry cell and the switch. Now you have completed the circuit.

8. Close the switch. What happens to the telegraph receiver? If nothing happens, you need to adjust the space between the arm of the metal Z and the nails. You might bring the metal arm a little closer to the nails. Open and close the switch a few times. Record your observations.

Time to Think ●

●   How does the telegraph set use electromagnetism? Can you use a circuit diagram for your explanation?

●   In 1844, the great American inventor and painter Samuel F. B. Morse (1791–1872) invented the telegraph, a device that made it possible to communicate with people in distant places much faster than ever before.

    The telegraph sends signals in the form of a code called the Morse code over electric wires. Obtain a copy of the Morse code. Find out how you can send a simple message on your telegraph by using the Morse code.

EXPERIMENT 37: How Do You Build a Buzzer?

Materials ● 6-volt cell, wood block, two large iron nails, switch, piece of metal (unpainted), noninsulated bell wire, screw, hammer

Procedure ● (see Figure 23)
Note: Instead of building another telegraph set, you can use the one you built for Experiment 36. However, you will have to modify the sounder, or telegraph receiver, to make it a buzzer.

1. Prepare the telegraph receiver as in steps 1 and 2 of Experiment 36. See the note above if you have already completed that experiment.
2. Hammer a tiny hole into the free end of the metal with a nail.
3. Connect a wire between one terminal of the cell and the hole of the metal arm.
4. Coil a long wire around one nail many times, working downward. Begin at the top of the nail and make sure that the free end of the wire sticks out from the top as shown. It is critical that the free end of this wire should lightly touch the free end of the metal as shown in the inset of Figure 23.
5. Bring the wire across to the other nail. Coil it around as many times as before, working upward.
6. Connect the other end of this wire to one terminal of the switch. Connect a second wire between the free terminal of the cell and the switch. Now you have made a complete circuit.
7. Close the switch. What happens? Continue to open and close the switch, and record your observations.

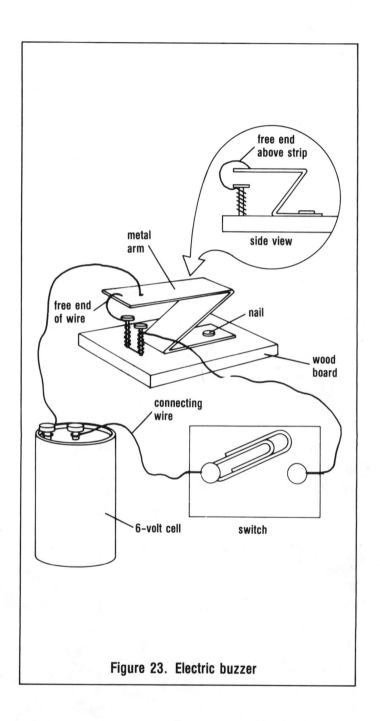

free end
above strip

side view

metal
arm

free end
of wire

nail

wood
board

connecting
wire

6-volt cell

switch

Figure 23. Electric buzzer

Time to Think ●

● How does the buzzer system work on electromagnetism? Can you use a circuit diagram to support your explanation?
● Predict what will happen if the free end of the wire from the nail is permanently connected to the free end of the metal arm. Can you support your prediction by what you know about an electric circuit and an electromagnetic circuit?

EXPERIMENT 38: How Do You Build a Simple Motor?

Materials ● Styrofoam cup, two paper clips, D cell, masking tape, two square magnets, thin enamel-covered wire (magnet wire), sandpaper

Procedure ● (see Figure 24)

1.   Coil the thin enamel-covered wire around your index finger four times. Pull the wire from your finger and you will get a wire loop. The two ends of the wire should extend from the loop at right angles as shown. Use a small piece of sandpaper to completely remove any coating on the ends of the wire. Set the loop aside.
2.   Bend two paper clips as shown to form a hook for supporting the wire loop horizontally.
3.   Tape the paper clips on each terminal of the cell in a vertical position. Check to see that the clips are equal in vertical length.
4.   Place the cell with the clips on the bottom of an inverted Styrofoam cup. Tape it down with masking tape.

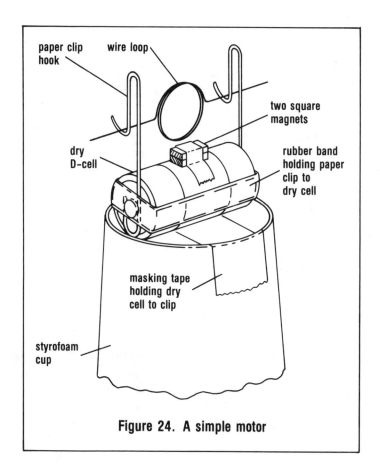

paper clip hook

wire loop

two square magnets

dry D-cell

rubber band holding paper clip to dry cell

masking tape holding dry cell to clip

styrofoam cup

Figure 24. A simple motor

5.   Tape two square magnets on the cell between the two clips.

6.   Place the wire loop gently on the paper clip hooks directly above, but not touching, the magnet. Make sure that everything is in a perfect horizontal position. Trial and error will tell you the best position. Record what happens.

● Examine the following components of the motor and its function. (1) The wire loop with the current flowing through it is the electromagnet. (2) The paper clips (hooks) deliver electricity to the wire loop. The hooks permit the wire loop to move or rotate. (3) The permanent square magnets interact with the electromagnet through repulsion and attraction.

After putting together the information from (1), (2), and (3), can you explain how the motor works on electromagnetism?

● Steam and running water are used to move an electric generator. There is a big motor inside the generator. Find out how a generator transforms mechanical energy to electric energy.

5

PROJECTS IN ELECTRICITY AND MAGNETISM

INTRODUCTION

Scientists have unique ways of solving problems—the scientific method of investigation. When scientists are confronted by a problem, they carefully set goals. Next, they collect background information on the subject by tedious research before actually pursuing the investigation. It is true that scientists sometimes make important discoveries by chance, but even these would be impossible without the scientists' special training and their ability to make sense of the accidental discovery.

HISTORY

Thomas A. Edison • Thomas A. Edison (1847–1931) epitomizes the spirit of American ingenuity. Edison is without a doubt America's most celebrated inventor and technologist. He owed his success in giving the world the incandescent carbon electric lamp and so many other important inventions not only to his genius but also to his remarkable persistence. Although his first attempts with various inventions often failed again and again, Edison always kept trying and learning from his failures until he eventually succeeded. He was issued a total of 1,093 patents.

Now that you have gained knowledge as well as skills in the basics of electricity and magnetism from the previous experiments, you are ready to go on to the next level of experiments and to more fun and challenging projects. You will have an opportunity to experience some exciting moments of Edison's actual work when you do Experiments 39 and 40, which replicate two of his investigations in electricity and magnetism.

EXPERIMENT 39: How Do You Make an Electric Light?

In Experiment 15 you investigated the inside of a light bulb. In this experiment you will actually make a light bulb yourself and thereby get an idea of how Thomas Edison must have felt when he invented the incandescent lamp in 1879.

Materials • 6-volt cell, insulated wires, copper-strand lamp wire, switch, small birthday candle, wide-mouth jar with lid, masking tape, soda bottle cap, match, hammer, nail

You can replicate two of the discoveries of the
great American inventor Thomas Alva Edison—the
electric light bulb and the relay telegraph—by doing
Experiments 39 and 40.

Procedure ●

1. Use the hammer and nail to make two small holes 4 to 5 cm apart in the lid of the wide-mouth jar. The best way to do this is to lay the lid (not the rim) flat on a board. Strip the ends of two wires and insert them into the jar. Bend the wires and tape them down on the lid with masking tape.

2. Remove one copper strand from the lamp wire. Coil it around a nail several times. Remove the coil. Connect the coil between the two wires from the lid.

3. Connect one wire from the lid to the terminal of the cell. Connect the other wire from the lid to the terminal of the switch. Connect another wire between the free terminal of the cell and the switch. You have now completed a circuit.

4. Place a lighted candle inside the jar using the soda bottle cap as the candle base. Screw in the lid tightly while the candle is still burning.

5. Close the switch to complete the circuit as soon as the flame goes out. Wait a few minutes. What happens? Record your observations. *Note:* this experiment is more dramatic if the last step is performed in a dark room.

Time to Think ●

● The experiment will also work without burning the candle. You can try that for comparison. What is the purpose of burning a candle inside the jar? (*Hint:* when the candle is out, what does it tell you about the air in the jar?)

- When you break a light bulb, it pops. What does that tell you about the inside of the bulb?
- What is inside a neon bulb? Why does it light up differently from an incandescent bulb?

EXPERIMENT 40: How Do You Build a Relay Telegraph System?

In Experiment 36 you had the opportunity to build a simple telegraph set. In Edison's time (around 1870) he found that the electric current flowing from a distant station was too weak to operate the electromagnet of the telegraph set. He therefore made an improvement of the old model and invented a relay system to boost the weak force and make it much stronger.

Materials • Strip of metal, small wood block, Popsicle stick, thumbtack, masking tape, iron screws, insulated wire, 6-volt cell, flashlight bulb and holder, 1.5-volt D cell, switch, sandpaper, solder and soldering iron (optional), hammer, nails

Procedure • (see Figure 25)
There are three major components to the relay telegraph system: the relay unit with the electromagnet, the low-voltage circuit, and the high-voltage circuit.

Relay Unit ○

1. Bend a metal strip in the form of a Z. Note that one end of the Z is longer. Secure the short end of the Z strip into the wooden block with a metal screw.

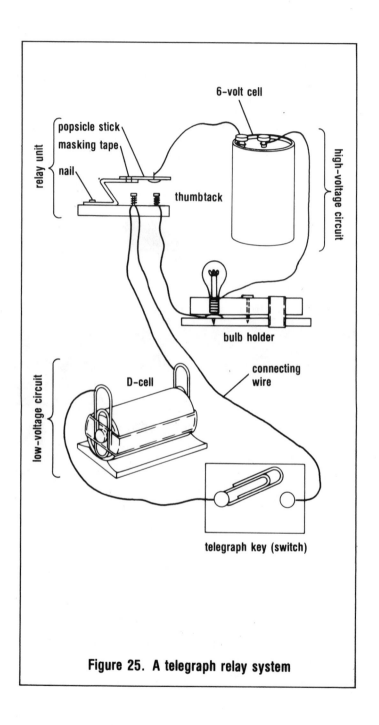

Figure 25. A telegraph relay system

2. Extend free arm of Z with a Popsicle stick and tape it down with masking tape. End of the Popsicle stick should not extend beyond the wooden block.

3. Press in a thumbtack near the end of the stick. Sand the head of the tack to ensure good conduction. You have just finished making the contact arm of the relay unit.

4. Hammer two nails onto the block. One nail should be located under the metal strip, the other directly under the thumbtack.

5. Coil about 100 turns of long insulated wire around the nail beneath the metal, leaving enough wire to make other wire connections. Twist the free ends together so the coil will not come apart. You have now made an electromagnet.

Low-Voltage Circuit ○

6. Connect one wire from the electromagnet of the relay unit to a 1.5-volt D cell.

7. Connect the D cell to one terminal of the telegraph key. The telegraph key is actually a modified switch.

8. Connect the second wire from the electromagnet to the other terminal of the telegraph key. Now you have made the low-voltage (1.5-volt) circuit and connected it to the relay unit.

High-Voltage Circuit ○

9. Connect a wire between the one terminal of the 6-volt cell and the thumbtack. You may choose to solder this connection since this is the moving part of the system. If you do, have an adult help you, and be careful not to inhale the harmful fumes from the soldering.

10. Connect the other terminal of the 6-volt cell to a 6-volt bulb. (*Note:* a flashlight bulb will burn out immediately with a 6-volt cell.)

11. Connect the third wire between the bulb holder and the nail beneath the thumbtack. Now you have completed the high-voltage circuit.

12. Depress the telegraph key. The closing of the key makes the low-voltage circuit complete. As you may recall, this represents a message coming in from a distant station. Open and close the key several times as if you were sending a telegraph message. Record what happens by completing the following chart.

Telegraph Components	What Happened?
Electromagnet	_____
Contact arm	_____
Light bulb	_____

Time to Think ●

● Draw a simple diagram to illustrate the flow of current in the low-voltage circuit and the high-voltage circuit.

● How was the low-voltage circuit used to control the high-voltage circuit by going through the relay unit? Can you explain?

● Which way is it easier for a telegraph operator to receive an incoming message: through the clicking of the contact arm or through the blinking of the light bulb?

EXPERIMENT 41: How Do You Build a Watchdog That Doesn't Eat or Sleep?

Anyone opening a door equipped with this "watchdog," which is actually an alarm, will be in for quite a surprise! You may want to take it anywhere you go; it is truly portable.

Materials ● 6-volt cell, two wood blocks, tape, electric doorbell, insulated wire, wooden clothespin, rubber bands, masking tape, eye screw, thumbtacks, hammer and nails, solder and soldering iron, string, sandpaper

Procedure ● (see Figure 26)
Like the circuits you have built earlier, the alarm basically consists of a power source (the cell) and power user (the bell) connected in a complete circuit with a set-off device (the switch).

1. Nail two wooden blocks together at a right angle. Place the 6-volt cell next to the upright block and secure it with rubber bands.
2. Place the doorbell flat on the horizontal board, next to the battery. You may want to nail it in place.
3. Place a wooden clothespin next to the doorbell. Tape it down in place. Push one thumbtack into each jaw of the pin. Make sure that the tacks are sanded to permit good conduction.
4. Place a piece of cardboard between the jaws of the clothespin. The cardboard is the insulator between the two thumbtacks. Attach a trip string to the cardboard. The other end of the trip string should be attached to the door.

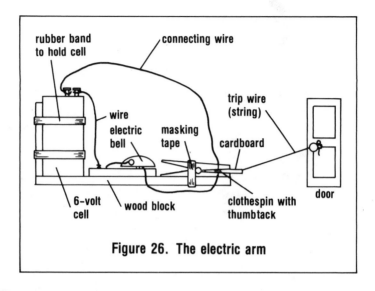

rubber band to hold cell

connecting wire

trip wire (string)

wire

electric bell

masking tape

cardboard

6-volt cell

wood block

clothespin with thumbtack

door

Figure 26. The electric arm

5.   Make the following wire connections:

•   From one terminal of the cell to one terminal of the bell
•   From the second terminal of the cell to one thumb-tack
•   From the other thumbtack to the second terminal of the doorbell.

6.   Put the alarm in place. The system is now ready to work for you.

7.   Have someone open the door. The door will pull on the trip string, which in turn will pull out the cardboard to permit direct contact between the two thumbtacks. Now you have a complete electric circuit. What happens?

- Make two simple diagrams to show the flow of electricity (1) when the cardboard was in place and (2) when the cardboard was pulled. Which of the two is the incomplete circuit? Which is the complete circuit?
- How would you make additional wire connections to include a flashlight bulb so that the light turns on at the same time the alarm bell rings?

UNITED STATES USE OF ELECTRICITY IS INCREASING

In recent years, 37 percent of the nation's energy has been used to produce electricity. Scientists predict that the figure will increase to 40 percent by the year 2000. The United States is becoming more and more dependent on electricity to meet its energy needs. In the past sixteen years the U.S. demand for electricity has grown by 45 percent, even though the population has grown by only 16 percent and our total demand for energy by only 8 percent.

To meet this increasing demand for electric power, a variety of energy sources are tapped. Some of those sources contribute a substantial amount of the electricity needed, while others contribute less than $\frac{1}{2}$ of 1 percent.

Do you know the major sources of this country's electricity? Can you rank them in order of their contribution to the U.S. demand for electricity?

The following nine sources were identified by a survey from the Energy Information Administration.

- *Biomass* energy results from the burning of wood and solid waste. This provides less than 0.1 percent of the nation's electricity.
- *Coal*. Eighty percent of the nation's coal output is used by electric utility companies to produce electricity. The burning of coal provides 57 percent of the nation's electricity.
- *Geothermal*. The use of geothermal energy, which is tapped from underground sources, is limited to the western United States. Geothermal energy produces 0.33 percent of the nation's electricity.
- *Hydropower*. Almost 10 percent of the nation's electricity is generated by running water. It is the leading renewable source used to provide electricity.
- *Natural Gas*. About half of the natural gas output was used by gas turbines to produce electricity during peak hours of demand. Natural gas produces 10 percent of the nation's electricity.
- *Uranium*. About 109 nuclear power stations presently provide the United States with almost 20 percent of its electrical needs.
- *Petroleum*. Six percent of the nation's electricity is provided by the use of petroleum.
- *Solar*. *Solar* energy provides about 0.0001 percent of the nation's electricity. The use of solar power is largely limited to certain geographic areas in the United States.
- *Wind* energy provides less than 0.0001 percent of the nation's electricity, and 95 percent of our wind-generated electricity is in the state of California.

U.S. ELECTRIC POWER GENERATION SOURCES

Sources	Rank
Coal	I
Uranium	2
Hydropower	3
Natural Gas	4
Petroleum	5
Geothermal	6
Biomass	7
Solar	8
Wind	9

More than half the electricity consumed in this country is generated by burning coal. Unfortunately, coal burning is also our main source of carbon dioxide gas pollution, which causes environmental problems such as global warming and a higher incidence of respiratory disease. As a result, more people are switching to using alternate sources of clean and renewable energy. Energy from the sun and wind seems to be the promising solution.

Scientists estimate that sunlight shining on the United States on a typical bright summer day can provide more energy than this country can use in two years! The problem is how to collect the energy and turn it into a usable form. Although solar energy has the potential of providing us with clean, renewable energy, it is unfortunately quite expensive to generate at present.

EXPERIMENT 42: How Do We Harness Electricity From the Sun?

Materials ● Block of wood, silicon solar cell (from electronic hobby store), magnet wire (no. 18), soldering iron and solder, tape, compass, two small alligator clips

Procedure ● (see Figure 27)

1.   Purchase a silicon solar cell from an electronic store. It is not expensive. You are all set if the solar cell comes with connecting wires. If it does, skip step 2, which deals with attaching those wires.

2.   Lay the solar cell faceup flat on a surface. Scrape the ends of two connecting wires. Put on safety glasses and gloves and, with adult supervision, solder a length of wire to the silver edge on the face of the cell. Turn the solar cell facedown and solder another length of wire to the silver surface anywhere on the back.

3.   Tape the solar cell and its connecting wires onto a block of wood as shown.

4.   Now place the solar cell aside and, unless you have already done so, build a simple galvanometer according to the directions in Experiment 33. A galvanometer is a sensitive instrument used to detect the presence of electricity.

5.   Connect the two wires from the solar cell to the wires of the galvanometer.

6.   Expose the solar light system to the following conditions and record your observations. Use the following chart to record your data.

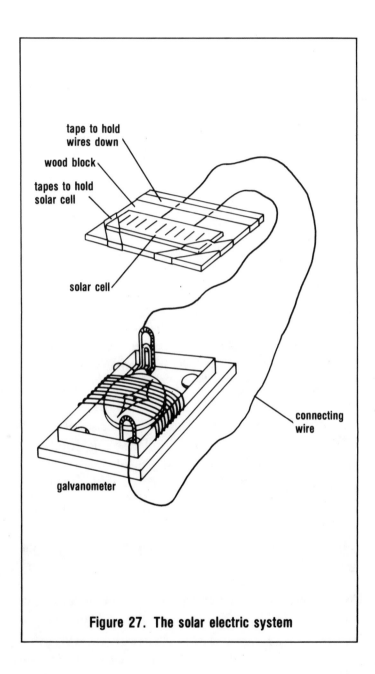

tape to hold
wires down

wood block

tapes to hold
solar cell

solar cell

connecting
wire

galvanometer

Figure 27. The solar electric system

Light Condition	Needle Deflection of the Galvanometer
Flashlight	_____
Direct sunlight	_____
Indirect sunlight (overcast)	_____
Incandescent light	_____
Fluorescent light	_____
Sunlamp light	_____

Time to Think •

• Look at your experiment data. Can you rank the movements of the galvanometer needle? What can you conclude about one disadvantage of using solar energy?

• Many space satellites use solar collectors to power their equipment. Find out (from the library) how solar collectors transform light into electricity.

• Have you ever used a solar calculator? Can you compare a solar calculator to a conventional dry-cell-operated calculator?

EXPERIMENT 43: How Do You Harness Electricity From the Wind?

Wind is related to the heat of the sun because air movement is caused by differences in air temperature, which result from solar heat. The concept of harnessing wind energy has been used since ancient times. Centuries ago

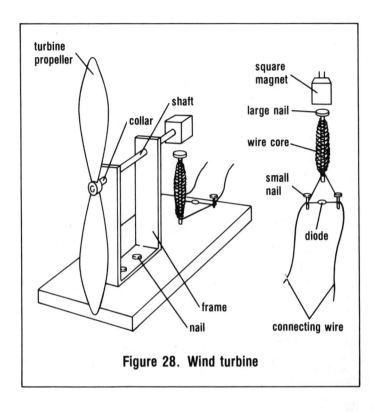

Figure 28. Wind turbine

wind was being used to propel sailing ships, to grind grain, and to pump water. Many scientists feel that in most locations the cost of converting wind energy to electricity would be too high at present to justify its use.

Materials ● Wood block, 6-inch (15.2-cm) model airplane propeller, large iron nails, smaller nails, small square magnet, metal strip, hammer, drill, magnet wire (no. 18), diode (1N34A) from an electronic hobby store, tape, solder and soldering iron, super-glue, electric tape

Procedure ● (see Figure 28) The wind electric generator has two major components: the turbine and the wire core. The turbine moves a magnet to push electrons in the wire core and thereby generate electricity.

Turbine ○

1. Glue the square magnet flat on the head of a large iron nail. Set it aside because it takes time for the glue to set. The nail is going to be the shaft of the turbine.

2. Prepare a tin can frame support as shown. Nail one end of the frame to the wood block.

3. Mark on the uprights of the frame where you will later drill holes for the shaft to go through. It is better to drill the holes later because you might need to change their position.

4. Attach the propeller to the other end of the nail when other parts of the system are ready to go.

Wire Core ○

5. Coil a long magnet wire around a large iron nail about 1,000 turns. The coil should be about 5 cm long. Leave two lengths of wire uncoiled for connections. Twist the ends of the wires together so they will not come apart.

6. Drive the nail into the wood block next to the upright of the turbine frame. The wire core standing up should be shorter than the frame upright. Hammer two smaller nails as shown in the wood with wires from the coil.

7. Put on safety glasses and work gloves. Solder a diode between the two small nails as shown. The pur-

pose of the diode is to convert the alternating current (AC) from the core to direct current (DC). DC is what you will use in the experiment.

8. Insert the shaft of the turbine through the frame. The bar magnet of the turbine must be directly above but not touching the head of the wire core when it moves. Wrap a collar of tape on the shaft as shown. This will prevent the shaft from sliding.

9. Carefully drill a small hole on the propeller and fit it snugly on the nail.

10. Expose the wind turbine to the wind or put it right in front of a fan. You may want to turn the blade of the propeller just to help it start.

11. The ultimate test of the system is to connect a light bulb or other test items to the two small nails. Use the following chart to record your data.

Test Items	What Happened to It?
Light bulb (1.5-volt)	_____
Light bulb (6-volt)	_____
Galvanometer (from Experiment 33)	_____
Heating wire	_____

Time to Think ●

● Based on your experiment data, what can you tell about the strength of the electric current generated by the wind turbine?

117

- Use your knowledge of electromagnetism to explain how electricity can be generated from the wind. (*Hint:* when the propeller spins, it also turns the magnet on the shaft. What will that turning magnet do to the wire core?)
- What other sources of energy can drive a turbine to generate electricity?

GLOSSARY

Alternating current. Electric current in which the flow of electrons reverses direction in regular cycles.

Amber. A hard, translucent fossil resin from pine trees. Amber, usually yellow or brown in color, is commonly used for carvings, jewelry, and electrical insulation.

Ammonium chloride. A white or colorless crystalline compound of ammonia that is commonly used in dry cells. The chemical formula for ammonium chloride is NH_4Cl.

Ampere. The standard unit of strength of an electric current. It is equal to the amount of current produced by 1 volt acting through a resistance of 1 ohm. The unit is named after the French physicist André Marie Ampère, 1775–1836.

Atom. The smallest particle of an element that has the chemical properties of that element. The atom has

119

a positively charged nucleus in the center surrounded by one or more negatively charged electrons.

Attraction. A force exerted by bodies on one another. The force tends to pull the bodies together.

Battery. Two or more electric cells connected together.

Biomass. That part of an environment consisting of living matter. Biomass is expressed either as the weight of organisms per unit area or as the volume of organisms per unit volume of the environment.

Circuit. A complete path through which an electric current passes.

Circuit breaker. An automatic switch which breaks the circuit when too much electricity is flowing. It is similar to a fuse, but, unlike a fuse, it can be reused.

Condenser. An electrical device that controls the supply of electricity by means of two plates that hold the electric charges.

Conductor. A substance that allows energy such as heat or electricity to pass through.

Crystal. A rock that is bounded by plane surfaces. Crystals are arranged in an orderly and repeated pattern. Sodium chloride, or table salt, is an example of a crystal.

Current. The flow of electricity in one direction.

Direct current. Electric current in which the flow of electrons goes in only one direction.

Dry cell. A combination of two metals in a chemical solution that produces electricity. Dry cells are used in flashlights and other devices.

Electric charge. A fundamental property of matter. An

electron carries a negative electric charge; a proton a positive electric charge.

Electric field. An area in which an electric charge experiences a force, as happens at the two anodes in the cathode ray tube of a television set.

Electricity. Energy carried by electrons, protons, and other subatomic particles. Electricity is capable of producing heat, light, and other effects.

Electric potential. The difference in electric pressures. The flow of electricity goes from a point of high electric potential to a point of low electric potential.

Electric resistance. The opposition to a flow of electricity. A substance that does not allow electricity to easily pass through has a high electric resistance.

Electrolyte. A solution which permits electric current to pass through.

Electromagnet. An iron core with insulated wire wound around it. The iron core becomes a magnet when electric current is supplied to the electric coil.

Electron. A subatomic particle that carries the smallest negative electric charge.

Electrophorus. A device for generating charges of static electricity by means of induction.

Electroplating. To apply a metal coating to the surface of an object by means of electrolysis.

Electroscope. An instrument used to detect and measure electric charges.

Electrostatics. A branch of physics that studies static electricity, or electricity at rest.

Flint. A hard, fine-grained stone that produces sparks when struck against steel. Flint is commonly used in cigarette lighters.

Friction. A force that resists motion between two surfaces that are in contact with one another.

Fuse. A safety device consisting of a strip of metal inserted in an electric circuit. The strip will melt and break the circuit if the electric current becomes excessive.

Galvanometer. An instrument for detecting and measuring the flow of electricity.

Generator. A machine that converts mechanical energy into electrical energy.

Geothermal. Related to the heat generated from the earth's interior.

Graphite. A soft, black crystalline carbon commonly used as a lubricant when mixed with oil and as "lead" for pencils. Graphite is a conductor of electricity.

Hypothesis. An educational guess or assumption based on known facts. A hypothesis can be used as a basis for further investigation and experimentation.

Igniter. A device that triggers burning, commonly used in cigarette lighters and gas grills.

Incandescent. Glowing with heat. An incandescent lamp is a light bulb in which light is produced by passing electric current through a thin high-resistance wire, causing it to glow.

Induction. The process of giving an electric charge to an object by bringing it close to a charged body.

Insulator. A material that prevents the flow of an electric current. Many nonmetals are insulators.

Ion. An atom whose outer electron shell has gained or lost one or more electrons. Positive ions are formed by the loss of electrons, negative ions by the gain of electrons.

Kilowatt-hour. A unit of electric energy indicating the amount of energy used at the rate of 1 kilowatt for 1 hour. Example: an electric heater takes electricity at the rate of 4 kilowatts.

Neon. A nonmetallic element that makes up a small percentage of the gases in air. Gaseous neon is used in electric lights. The chemical symbol for neon is Ne.

Neutral. In electricity, neither positively nor negatively charged.

Neutron. An elementary particle in the atom that has no electric charge.

Nichrome. A metallic substance with very high electrical resistance. Because of that unique property, nichrome wire is used as heating elements in such appliances as toasters and heaters.

Nucleus. The positively charged center of the atom. The nucleus consists of protons and neutrons.

Parallel circuit. An electric circuit in which two or more components (for example, the electric source and the electric user) are arranged in the same direction in parallel positions relative to each other.

Piezoelectricity. Electricity generated by the action of certain crystals showing negative and positive electric charges under mechanical pressure.

Polarization. The state of having two opposing forces or positions.

Quartz. A very hard form of silica that occurs in crystalline form. Quartz is the most common of all minerals and is the principal component of sand.

Repulsion. The force exerted by two bodies pushing away from each other.

Rheostat. An electrical device for changing the resistance of a circuit. Rheostats are commonly used for dimming lights.

Semiconductor. A solid whose conductivity is less than a conductor's and more than an insulator's.

Series circuit. An electric circuit in which the components (for example, the electric source and the electric user) are arranged in a linear fashion, positioned one after another.

Silicon. A nonmetallic element that exists in its pure state as either brown powder or dark-gray crystals. Silicon is the second most abundant element in the earth's crust. The chemical symbol for silicon is Si.

Solar. Relating to the sun.

Tourmaline. A glassy crystal of complex composition. It is often used as a semiprecious stone.

Ultrasonic. Relating to sound waves having a frequency beyond the range audible to human beings. Ultrasonic sound is usually above 20,000 cycles per second.

Uranium. A heavy silvery element with many forms, some of which are used in the production of nuclear fuel.

Volt. A unit for measuring electric pressure or force. One volt consists of the amount of electric pressure needed to produce 1 ampere of electric current where the resistance of the material carrying the current is 1 ohm.

Watt. A unit for measuring electric power. One watt is equal to 1 joule of work per second.

FOR FURTHER READING

Ardley, Neil. *Discovering Electricity.* New York: Franklin Watts, 1984.

———. *The Science Book of Electricity.* San Diego: Harcourt Brace Jovanovich, 1991.

Asimov, Isaac. *How Did We Find Out About Electricity?* New York: Walker, 1973.

Berger, Melvin. *Switch On, Switch Off.* New York: Crowell, 1989.

Graf, Rudolph. *Safe and Simple Electrical Experiments.* New York: Dover Publications, 1984.

Gutnik, Martin J. *Electricity: From Faraday to Solar Generators.* New York: Franklin Watts, 1986.

Taylor, Barbara. *Electricity and Magnets.* New York: Franklin Watts, 1990.

Wood, Robert. *Physics for Kids: 49 Easy Experiments with Electricity and Magnetism.* Blue Ridge Summit, Pa.: Tab Books, 1990.

INDEX